Charminar

Foreword

I have been in and out of Hyderabad since 1984 and this is where I love coming back to. The art and aesthetics, the history and culture, the endearing language and the rhythm of life here are all very close to my heart. The cultural and historical portrait of the city aims at showing Hyderabad in all its diversity – its communities, traditions and culture where people enjoy to live, share and celebrate life .

In this book, I offer vignettes from the lives of the people and events that have shaped the city's history interlaced with tales of romance, intrigue, war and victory. Also proffered is a sliver of everyday life – the rituals and routines that make Hyderabad so special.

Noopur Kumar

Paigah Tombs

Acknowledgments

This book would not have been possible without the support of my parents and my family. I would like to thank Mr Zahid Ali Khan, Editor Siyasat, for lending some incredible pictures from the Siyasat library. I express my gratitude to Mr P Narendra for his valuable advice and support throughout. I want to thank Mr AN Medhora and Mrs Katy Medhora for gladly sharing their memorabilia and memories with me. I acknowledge with gratitude, the support of Mr G Kishan Rao. I am grateful to Mr H Rajendra Prasad, Mr D Chandrasekhar Reddy and Mr K Chakrapani for graciously reviewing the manuscript and providing valuable inputs. I can never forget the evenings spent with Nawab Mahboob Alam Khan as we sampled his cooking and listened to him trace the culinary culture of the city. I am appreciative of the support and contribution of Mr AKVS Reddy, former Director SalarJung Museum, Dr A Nagender Reddy, Director Salarjung Museum and the Commissioner Dept. of Archives, Govt. of A.P. Thank you, Brigadier V Sriramulu (Retd), Brigadier YV Mohan, Commandent EME Center, Air Commodore R Kacker, VM and Squadron Leader Shivika Khanna for all your help. I would like to thank Mr Jagdish Mittal for sharing some beautiful pictures from the Jagdish and Kamla Mittal Museum of Indian Art.

I would like to thank the young and creative Mr V Janardhan and Mr P Narsimha Murthy of Ravi Press for their help. In the end, I would like to thank Mr D Ravinder Reddy, for his amazing pictures that made all the difference to this book.

Noopur Kumar

The High Court

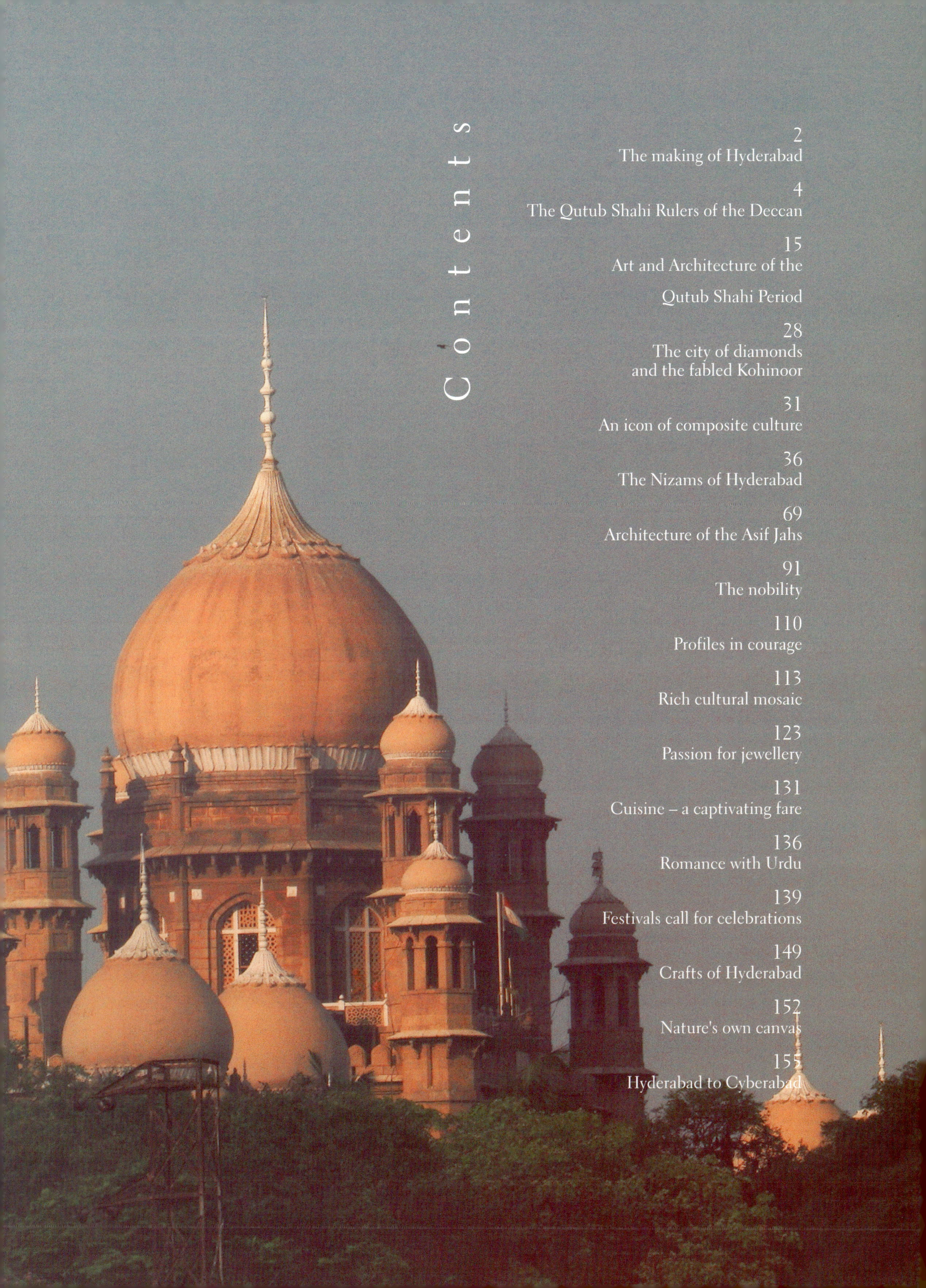

Contents

Muhammad Quli Qutub Shah & Bhagmati

THE MAKING OF HYDERABAD

The city of Hyderabad was born out of love - the love of a feisty young Muslim prince for a Hindu woman. If the Mughal King Shahjahan built the greatest monument of love - the Taj Mahal for his wife Mumtaz, Muhammad Quli Qutub Shah built the city of Hyderabad for Bhagmati. An abiding motif of its times, Hyderabad is not just a city but a journey - a quest of a passionate soul who attempted to reaffirm the dignity of love that transcends faith and religion. A great builder, philosopher and a benevolent monarch, Muhammad Quli firmly believed that the city of Hyderabad would be an embodiment of peace, freedom and compassion. An architectural icon, the city presents a rich tapestry of myriad hues where style met scale, tradition wed modernity and inspiration fused with structural splendour to make a visionary's dream come true.

The fourteen year old crown prince of Golconda, Muhammad Quli Qutub Shah was madly in love with Bhagmati, a beautiful Hindu courtesan. Every evening, the besotted lover would ride to the village of Chichlam across river Musi, to meet his beloved, for he couldn't live without watching her dance, oh so gracefully, and sing in that soulful voice of hers!

Legend has it that once heavy rains and thunderstorm lashed Golconda and the city was devastated. The Musi River was in spate, destroying homes and lives. Muhammad Quli Qutub Shah could not bear to be away from Bhagmati in this hour and decided to cross the flooded river. His bodyguards tried to dissuade the lovelorn prince, but in vain. It was a dark night and braving the raging torrent, the prince rode to the shore of the river. He coerced his hesitant horse to step into the river and as soon as it did, a furious current nearly swept it away. It was a miracle that both survived and reached the other end. Muhammad Quli rode towards Chichlam to meet Bhagmati. Most of the homes in the vicinity were destroyed in the deluge and he feared for her safety. To his luck, Bhagmati was alive and after the storm weakened, they left together for Golconda.

When Sultan Ibrahim, the father of the young prince heard this tale of dangerous passion that almost killed his dear son, he was alarmed and forbade him from meeting Bhagmati. The prince was miserable without her. Beautiful women from Arabia, Persia, Armenia and different parts of India were brought to amuse the prince, but none could lure him away from his beloved. Muhammad Quli loved Bhagmati and no woman, no matter how beautiful, could take her place. The Sultan relented and the doting father even constructed the *Purana Pul* – a massive stone bridge across the Musi River, to make it easy for the young prince to reach Chichlam.

Bhagmati

The romance of the crown prince with a dancer evoked great curiosity and controversy in Golconda. The fact that Bhagmati was a Hindu and much older than the prince, created quite a scandal as no one was ready to accept her as queen. After ascending the throne, Muhammad Quli Qutub Shah defied all traditions, married Bhagmati, made her his queen and she bore his only child, Hayat Bakshi Begum.

Muhammad Quli was a great builder and in the year 1591, laid the foundation of a new city which he called Bhagnagar after his beloved queen. Bhagmati later embraced Islam and took the name Hyder Mahal and Bhagnagar was renamed Hyderabad after her.

THE QUTUB SHAHI RULERS OF THE DECCAN

Sultan Quli Qutub Shah

(Accession 1518 – Death 1543)

The Qutub Shahi dynasty was founded by Sultan Quli Qutub Shah whose ancestors belonged to the Turkman tribe of Hamadan in Iran. He steadily rose to power and became the Governor of Golconda. After the Bahamani power disintegrated in the Deccan, Quli Qutub Shah strengthened his control over his domain. Following the trend of the other five *subedars* (governors) of the Bahamani kingdom, he proclaimed his independence and established a new dynasty of the Qutub Shahis with Golconda as the capital .

Between leading successful expeditions and subjugating the rebellious *zamindars* (landlords) of Telangana, Sultan Ibrahim Quli

Golconda

continued to fortify his capital. He reinforced the old mud structure at Mankal in Golconda with granite and created an invincible citadel that would be the symbol of his absolute power over the Deccan. He revamped the fortress capital by adding new mosques, impressive palaces and beautiful gardens. The Jame Masjid near the Bala Hissar entrance of the fort was built during his reign and the Persian inscription at the entrance bears his name. Sultan Quli reigned for twenty three years as the governor and twenty five years as the Sultan of Golconda. He was in his seventies when he became the king of Golconda.

In 1543, at the ripe age of ninety nine he was assassinated by Mir Mahmood Hamdani, the keeper of the fort, at the behest of his own son, Jamshid Quli, who was desperate to usurp the throne.

Jamshid Quli

Jamshid Quli

(Accession 1543 – Death 1550)

Jamshid Quli reigned for seven turbulent years. The fledgling kingdom was shocked at his action and refused to accept a sovereign guilty of patricide. Ill health led to his death in 1550.

Subhan Quli

(Accession 1550 – Dethroned 1550)

Jamshid Quli's seven year old son, Subhan Quli, was crowned by the queen and her political advisors, mainly a few Persian nobles in the court. Civil strife and anarchy ensued and the young Subhan was replaced by another insignificant ruler, Daulat Quli. He met an untimely death and was succeeded by Ibrahim Quli Qutub Shah.

The Charminar

Ibrahim Quli Qutub Shah

(Accession 1550 – Death 1580)

Ibrahim Quli Qutub Shah, the youngest son of Sultan Quli Qutub Shah was crowned the king of Golconda. All this while when Golconda was in turmoil, Ibrahim Quli was living in exile in the kingdom of Vijaynagar and was accorded a warm welcome when he reached Golconda. He married Bhagirathi, the Hindu princess of Vijayanagar.

Ibrahim Quli Qutub Shah was one of the most important rulers of the Qutub Shahi regime. To him goes the credit of strengthening the kingdom which had been enfeebled by dissension, rebellion, intrigue and weak rulers. He laid a strong foundation for the dynasty by providing able administration and tolerance towards religious and social diversity besides promoting trade, art and culture. The ceremonies, rituals, exotic food and other interesting facets of *Hyderabadi* tradition seen today, can be attributed to the cultural enrichment during the reign of Sultan Ibrahim. His early years in the kingdom of Vijaynagar had taught him to speak and write good Telugu. The language received great patronage under him and *farmans* or orders were often issued in Telugu for the benefit of the local population. Patrons of both Urdu and Telugu literature were honoured in the court. Hindu officials were appointed to crucial military, diplomatic and administrative positions, reflecting his acceptance and tolerance for all communities.

During Ibrahim Quli's reign, Golconda became an important center for international trade attracting traders from Turkistan, Arabia and

Persia. The fort at Golconda was strengthened with stone and mortar and an alms house and a black platform called the *Kala Chabutra* were built. Roads were widened and mosques, schools, tanks, gardens, baths and shops were built within the fortress town. Though it was his son Muhammad Quli who ultimately founded the city of Hyderabad, it was Sultan Ibrahim who initiated the plan for a new city. The growing population of the fort had begun to put a strain on the civic amenities in the area and the threat of disease began to loom large.

As life within the fort was too crowded, the Sultan encouraged the town to expand westwards. In 1578, he had the Purana Pul built across the Musi to ease the traffic within the city and to encourage settlement across the river. It was Ibrahim Quli who ordered the excavation of the Hussain Sagar Lake to be used to irrigate the farmland around the city. After providing thirty

jewellers in the city, some even from Persia and Armenia. Abbe Carre, a visitor to the city in 1672-74, also remarked on the flourishing trade in diamonds, pearls, steel and fabric by the local and foreign merchants in Hyderabad and called it 'the center of all trades in the east'. Hyderabad soon outgrew Golconda and became a hub of all cultural, intellectual and commercial activity.

Twenty five years after the founding of Hyderabad, an observation made in *Tarekh-i-Qutb Shahi* says,

The city is verily a paradise,
There is nothing that is not
to be found here.

If an old man hurries to the city
He would recover his youth.

Everything that is good is found in
Hyderabad in plenty,

We find in the city all that is fortunate and nothing that causes pain or sorrow.....

With time the city became a melting pot where different people, languages, ethnicity and rituals blended to create an extremely tolerant and multihued culture.

In January 1612, at the young age of forty six, Muhammad Quli passed away. The dynastic history of the Qutub Shahi rulers reached its pinnacle during the reign of Muhammad Quli Qutub Shah.

Sultan Muhammad Qutub Shah
(Accession 1612 – Death 1626)

The next ruler was Muhammad Quli's nephew Muhammad Qutub Shah. He was married to

Muhammad Quli's only daughter Begum Hayat Bakshi. An extremely pious man, he laid the foundation of the Mecca Masjid in 1617. He was ably assisted in the administration of the city by his minister, Mir Momin. When Mir Momin passed away, Begum Hayat Bakshi played an important role guiding her husband in matters of the state. He also planned another city, Sultan Nagar, to the east of Hyderabad. However, due to his untimely death in 1626, the plan never took off.

Abdullah Qutub Shah

(Accession 1626 – Death 1672)

Abdullah Qutub Shah was barely twelve years old when he ascended the throne and his mother, Begum Hayat Bakshi, administered the state on behalf of the minor king. Later, the king was so totally engrossed in pleasurable pursuits that he could spare little time for administrative matters. Twice, the kingdom came under attack from the Mughals. Abdullah Qutub Shah passed away in 1672 .

Abdullah Qutub Shah

Abul Hasan Tana Shah

(Accession 1672 – Death 1699)

The next to ascend the throne was Abdullah Qutub Shah's son-in-law, Abul Hasan Tana Shah. The last ruler of the Qutub Shahi dynasty, Tana Shah was a benevolent ruler and a valiant warrior who fought bravely to defend Golconda which in recent times had become a target of incessant Mughal attacks. Golconda's wealth and its legendary diamonds attracted the Mughals and in 1687, Aurungzeb attacked Golconda and laid siege for nearly eight months.

The tale of the *Kagaz Burj* or the Paper Bastion

During the course of the siege, Aurungzeb's army targeted a section of the massive fortress wall and a portion of it was blown away. The Sultan realized that it was impossible to repair the damage overnight. Not to give up easily, he asked his artisans to work all night and reconstruct the bastion with paper and cardboard. The mock-up job was perfectly executed and completely deceived the Mughal army. The Mughal Emperor was crestfallen.

Abul Hasan Tana Shah

Even today this portion of the bastion is known as *Kagaz Burj* or the Paper Bastion.

Treason, has led to the downfall of many kingdoms including Golconda. Abdullah Khan Puni, a treacherous general in the Qutub Shahi army, secretly sent word to Aurungzeb that if he promised him the governorship of Deccan, he would ensure that the doors of the fort were left open. Aurungzeb was more than happy to make the promise. September 21, 1687 was the fateful day when Golconda fell to deceit. The gate was opened by one of the unfaithful guards and the Mughal army rushed in, taking the residents by surprise. After eight months of valiant resistance, the city fell into the hands of the Mughals. Abul Hasan Tana Shah, the last king of Golconda, was imprisoned at Daulatabad where twelve years later, he died in captivity.

The tale of Bhakta Ramdas

Any discussion about the reign of Sultan Abul Hasan Tana Shah would be incomplete without a mention of the legend of Bhakta Ramdas. The story goes that a government official, named Gopanna served in the village of Bhadrachalam which was a part of the kingdom of Golconda. He was a devotee of Lord Rama and was popularly known as Bhakta Ramdas. He was so blinded in his devotion that he built a temple of Lord Rama for which he drew six hundred thousand rupees from government funds. When the Sultan heard of the misappropriation, he was furious. Ramdas was taken into custody and imprisoned at Golconda.

The devout Ramdas etched images of Lord Rama on the walls of his cell and prayed. Nothing could come between him and the Lord. One day a handsome young man came to the Sultan, handed him a bag with 600,000 gold coins and requested the Sultan to set Ramdas free. No one knew who he was. Ramdas was a free man but he was convinced it was Lord Rama who had come to his rescue. The Muslim king was moved by the dedication of Ramdas and offered pearls and jewellery to the diety at Bhadrachalam.

On September 22, 1687, Golconda was conquered by Aurungzeb and became a part of the six Mughal provinces in the Deccan. Mahabat Khan who was initially the Commander of the Golconda army, now joined the Mughal camp. He was appointed the Governor of Golconda-Hyderabad state, by Aurungzeb. Though Aurungzeb tried to consolidate his authority over Hyderabad, the city began to lose its importance. The final nail was struck when the capital of the new province was shifted from Hyderabad to Aurangabad, which became the new headquarters of the Mughals in the Deccan.

Between the fall of the Qutub Shahi dynasty and the rise of the Asif Jahis, Hyderabad suffered. Aurungzeb's only contribution to the city was the completion of the Mecca Masjid in 1693. In 1763, nearly seventy six years later, Hyderabad regained its lost glory when Nizam Ali Khan, the second Asif Jahi ruler moved the capital back from Aurungabad to Hyderabad.

The Charminar

ART AND ARCHITECTURE OF THE QUTUB SHAHI PERIOD

Charminar seen through Lad Bazar, 19th Century

The Charminar

Goethe described architecture as frozen music; if so then Charminar is melody set in concrete. The soul and symbol of Hyderabad, it is to Hyderabad what Taj is to Agra, the Gateway of India to Mumbai and the Qutub to Delhi! Often called the 'Arc de Triomphe of the East', Hyderabad is best represented by Charminar or 'the monument with four minarets' as it literally means.

The Charminar, by far the most remarkable architectural monument in the kingdom of Golconda was built in the year 1590-91, by the illustrious Muhammad Quli Qutub Shah. According to the author of the *Tuzuk-i-Qutub Shahi*, the Charminar was one of the first monuments erected when the foundation of the city was being laid. It bears a strong likeness to the tomb of one of Prophet Mohammad's grandsons Hazrat Imam Raza in Khorasan, Iran.

Why was the Charminar built? Historians have yet to reach a consensus on the reason for the construction of this grand edifice. Many hold the view that it was built to celebrate the end of plague – an epidemic that had killed thousands in the kingdom. The desperate king knelt and begged *Allah* to put an end to the misery of his people. Miraculously, a few days later the epidemic ebbed and the king thanked the Almighty. He vowed to erect a splendid structure on the very site where he had knelt and pleaded for God's mercy. Thus was built the Charminar – a truly inspired piece of architecture!

The city of Hyderabad was planned in the shape of a giant double cross. The Charminar stood at the city center, at the intersection of the existing highway running from Golconda in the west to Masulipatnam in the east and a new road running from the north of the kingdom to the extreme south.

The architectural plan of the structure shows precision and symmetry. It is a perfect square with each side measuring 20 meters. There are four lofty arched openings on each of the four sides which are 11meters wide and 20 meters high. The *Minars* or the towers have four storeys and rise 54 meters above the street level. Steep stone stairs lead up to the monument's upper floors. The terrace offers a panoramic view of the entire city - the chaotic old town around the Musi River, the glossy high rises of the new city and the relics of the magnificent Golconda fort receding into the skyline. The fine stucco facade in light ochre with intricate pattern, exemplifies the fine workmanship of the Qutub Shahi period. Large quantities of egg white were used to give the walls a smooth and creamy texture.

The Charminar was not just intended to be an exquisite piece of architecture that would adorn the city eternally, but also serve a purpose. The

Charminar seen through Lad Bazar, today

western side of the roof on the second floor houses a beautiful mosque built by the most competent of the Qutub Shahi artisans. It has forty five prayer areas and a large open space in front to accommodate a larger congregation on Fridays when the Muslims assemble for special prayers. The first storey also has a *Madarsa* or a school for Muslim chidren. The ramparts of the Charminar were used to make important proclamations like the accession of kings and later the Nizams. Mir Osman Ali Khan's coronation in 1911 was the last proclamation made from this imposing bulwark.

It is estimated that the overall cost of construction of the Charminar was a whopping Rs 700,000 – an enormous sum back then. When Golconda was sieged in 1687, one of the minarets was struck by lightning and severely damaged. The repair of the minaret cost sixty thousand rupees.

Chronicles confirm that Charminar was also besieged by enemies a couple of times when General Bussy and his men laid siege to the monument in 1756 and again in 1884 when guards of the Afghan city police were stationed here. Legend has it that the design and execution of this architectural marvel were so widely appreciated that the Sultan fearing plagiarization had the drawings of the building destroyed and the architects and artisans thrown to death from the top floor of one of the minarets!

Today the Charminar stands in quiet dignity, towering above the cacophony of the old city and other Qutub Shahi edifices in the vicinity - a silent testimony to the eventful saga of a four hundred year old city!

Golconda Fort

In 1143, during the reign of the Kakatiyas of Warangal, a shepherd boy found an idol on a rocky hill called Mankal. He went and showed it to the king. The king was so impressed with the find that he built a mud fort around the spot and renamed the place Golconda - derived from the Telugu word *Gollakonda* or the hill of the shepherds.

During the reign of Sultan Muhammad Shah Bahmani, Raja Krishna Deva of Warangal handed over the mud fortress of Mankal to the Sultan who named it Muhammadnagar after himself and made it an important fort of the Bahmani kingdom. Crowning an isolated granite hill, the fort rises 400 feet above the surrounding plain and is protected by a girdle of hills. Actually, there are three concentric fortifications, defending the citadel of Bala Hissar that forms the apex of the fortress. The Bala Hissar stood on a bed of solid granite and commanded a panoramic view of the city. It was the womb of the fortress where the king could confine himself in desperate times as there was a well of water, place for storing magazines and gun powder and numerous granaries hollowed out of the bedrock.

Three walls encircle the fort, their thickness varying from seventeen to thirty four feet. The walls are interrupted by eighty seven semi circular bastions, fifty to sixty feet high, carved out of huge blocks of granite. The three most famous of the bastions are the Petla, Musa and the Madina Burj. The famous *Fateh Rahbar* gun or 'the harbinger of victory' is positioned on the Petla Burj.

There are eight *Darwazas* (gates) in the outer wall: the Fateh, Bahmani, Mecca, Patancheru, Banjara, Jamali, Naya Quila and Moti Gates. The *Fatah Darwaza* (victory gate) is the most important of all the gates and is thirteen feet wide and twenty five feet high. The beautifully carved heavy teak doors were studded with spikes to prevent elephants from battering the gates. Sliding wooden planks were used to close the door from inside as a measure of precaution in times of war when drunken elephants were cajoled to pummel at the gates. There is an inner gate within this, similar in shape and size but devoid of the spikes. Even today, cannon balls are piled up near the gates. It was through the Fatah Darwaza that the triumphant Mughal army under Prince Moazzam marched into the fort.

A unique signaling device was incorporated into the construction of the fort. The different structures were so built that they deflected sound to different points within the fort. You could stand at the entrance foyer and clap and the sound would get carried to the hill top.

The Jame Masjid, the *Ashur Khana* or the house of mourning , *Naya Quila* or the 'New Fort', *Aslah Khana* or the armoury, *Ambar Khana* or the treasury and the *Katora Hauz-* a stone and mortar tank believed to be the largest of its kind in the world, are the important surviving monuments within Golconda.

Street cricket outside Golconda

Visitors at the Golconda Fort

The Mecca Masjid

Mecca Masjid is the second largest mosque in the country and the seventh largest in the world. Bricks were brought all the way from Mecca to build the central arch of this mosque and thus it got its name. Friday prayers still bring in more than ten thousand devout Muslims to this mosque.

The Qutub Shahi rulers built a large number of mosques in and around the capital, the most renowned of which were the Jami Masjid near the Golconda Fort, a mosque on top of the Charminar, the Syedabad Mosque, Mirpet Mosque, Hayat Bakshi Begum's Mosque and the Mushirabad Mosque. But one mosque that towers above all is the Mecca Masjid near Charminar. Work was initiated in 1614 by Sultan Muhammad Quli Qutub Shah and the mosque was completed seventy seven years later by the Mughal Emperor, Aurungzeb. A solemn structure devoid of superfluities, it has classic

proportions. The prayer hall is two hundred and twenty five feet long, one hundred and eighty feet wide and seventy five feet high. The structure has five huge openings capped by elegant arches. The six stone pillars supporting these arches are thirty feet high, seven and a half feet wide and carved out of single stones.

Travernier, who visited the city when the *Masjid* was under construction wrote in his travelogue, 'About fifty years since they began to build a magnificent *masjid* in the city which would have been the finest in India had it been finished wherein the niche is made where they say their prayers (*mihrab*), in an entire rock of such prodigious bulk that it was five years before five or six thousand men, continuously employed, could heave it out of its place. It was rolled on an engine with wheels upon which they brought it to the Pagoda, and several affirmed to me that there were fourteen hundred oxen to draw it.' As many as two thousand stone cutters, two thousand masons and a workforce of four thousand men laboured on this project for several years to complete it. An interesting departure from the other structures of this period was the use of dressed stones instead of stucco on the front facade.

The Qutub Shahi Tombs

Situated outside the northern wall of Golconda, is the royal necropolis of the Qutub Shahi rulers. Exhibiting great elegance, these tombs are a picture of perfect symmetry and yet another reminder of the splendour of the Qutub Shahi architecture. They can be reached by flights of steps and beautiful arcades and arches add to the grace of the entire structure.

There are thirty tombs in all among which the most significant are the tombs of the seven Qutub Shahi kings. The tomb of the last king of the regime, Sultan Abul Hasan Tana Shah is in Daulatabad where he died in captivity. The most beautiful of all the tombs is that of Begum Hayat Bakshi, daughter of Muhammad Quli Qutub Shah. Also to be found are tombs of important officers, members of the royal family, royal physicians and other associates of the royal family .

Inside a tomb

Though homogenous in appearance, the sizes of the tombs vary considerably. They are all square chambers perched on raised plinths and surrounded by colonnades. Pinnacled domes placed on lotus petals form coronets for the structure. Little minarets and stucco embellishments have been added to soften the solidity of the grey granite stones used for the construction.

The mausoleum rests in the midst of a beautifully laid out garden called the Ibrahim Bagh filled with groves of fruit laden trees, flowering bushes, fountains and cascades all meticulously planned to impart a serene ambience to the burial site.

Hussain Sagar

The Husain Sagar was excavated in 1562 during the reign of Ibrahim Qutub Shah . This lake was created by Hazrat Hussain Shah Wali, son-in-law of Ibrahim Quli Qutub Shah, to meet the water and irrigation needs of the city and was named after him. A one and a half mile bund, known as Tank Bund, at one end of the lake links the two cities of Hyderabad and Secunderabad.

The Purana Pul

The Purana Pul or the old bridge is the most famous of the four bridges of Hyderabad and was built by Sultan Ibrahim Qutub Shah. Around six hundred feet long, thirty five feet wide and fifty four feet above the river bed, the bridge has twenty two arched spans to support it. It was built by the Sultan for

Hussain Sagar

his love-stricken son Muhammad Quli. The bridge facilitated the spread of the city beyond the fortress of Golconda.

The Darul Shifa

The Darul Shifa (the house of healing) was built in 1595-96 by Muhammad Quli Qutub Shah who had planned the construction of a large number for buildings of public utility in his newly laid city. This was a teaching hospital where all were welcome for free medical assistance. It was an important center for *Unani* medicine – a natural system of medicine derived from ancient Greek healing methods. Students from Greece, Italy and even the Persian Gulf came here to study Unani medicine. One of the largest hospitals of its time, it could accommodate four hundred patients. *Sartuq* or a standard made of steel which supposedly possessed healing powers, stood in the courtyard. Many believers thronged here for spiritual healing.

Taramati Baradari

The romance of Taramati and Abdullah Qutub Shah, the seventh Sultan, created quite a stir in the fortress town of Golconda. Taramati was a beautiful singer and danseuse in the court of Abdullah Qutub Shah and the Sultan was besotted with her charm and her magical voice. The Sultan built a Baradari or a pavilion with twelve doors for his favourite courtesan from where music flowed every evening. Taramati would sing at the marquee and the Sultan would hear her soulful voice while he rested in his palace at Golconda, a mile away.

In the year 2004, Taramati Baradari was restored to its old glory. With an amphitheater, restaurant and a Convention Center, the Baradari today has come alive. Music, dances and *chowki* dinners organized here bring back the memory of the magical saga of the romance of Taramati and Abdullah Qutub Shah.

Sadly, very few of the structures of the Qutub Shahi times survive today. Time and apathy have taken their toll. The grand *Havelis* with their intricately carved minarets and arcades are in a state of decay or have been razed to the ground by unconcerned citizens who failed to realize the worth of these priceless pieces of history.

THE CITY OF DIAMONDS AND THE FABLED KOHINOOR

Southern India has figured prominently in Kautilya's Arthashastra and Ptolemy's Geography for its amazing wealth of gold and precious stones. It enjoyed prolific trading ties with the Roman Empire for reasons none other than its abundant treasure of gold, pearls and diamonds.

Until 1725, when diamonds were discovered in Brazil, the diamond mines near Golconda gave the world such celebrated pieces as the Kohinoor, the Great Mughal, the Pitt or Regent, the Orloff and the Hope diamond – all of which were taken from the country of their origin. Golconda was a virtual El Dorado and the diamond capital of the world. Thevenot, a French traveller who visited India in the middle of the 17th century referred to it as 'the country of diamonds'. During the Qutub Shahi reign, Golconda was one of the leading markets of diamonds. 'Seeing the city of Golconda is like seeing the city of diamonds', is how a visitor once described the city.

The Karwan area of the city grew into a thriving business center where diamonds were cut, polished and traded. Diamond traders and dealers both local and from abroad thronged to Golconda. The diamond mine spread over an area of fifty thousand square kilometers and the actual mining was done in Kollur, in the modern day Krishna Pennar basin to the east of the Deccan plateau. Tavernier visited Kollur during this time and mentioned that some of the stones mined here weighed more than forty carats.

Diamond dealers were very wealthy and one such merchant was Mir Jumla who later became the Prime Minister of Golconda. He is said to be the richest man in the Deccan, second only to the king. The world famous Kohinoor was excavated from the Kollur mines and belonged to Mir Jumla, the Prime Minister and commander-in-chief of Abdullah Qutub Shah. When Sultan Abdullah Qutub Shah tried to curb his Prime Minister's growing power, Mir Jumla defected and joined hands with the Mughals. To please the Mughal Emperor Shah Jahan, Mir Jumla gifted him the precious stone that weighed a whopping two hundred and forty carats then.

In 1665, Tavernier saw the Kohinoor in Aurungzeb's court and gave an account of the amazing stone. Due to the blunder of a Venetian jeweller, Hortensio Borgio, who ground the stone instead of cutting it, the weight of the stone was considerably reduced . For this folly he was fined ten thousand rupees – a considerable sum during those days! In 1739 the notorious Persian ruler Nadir Shah invaded Delhi, defeated Aurungzeb's feeble descendent, Muhammad Shah and took the Kohinoor away to Persia. When Nadir Shah first saw the stone he was stunned by its radiance and exclaimed, 'Koh-i-noor' which meant – the mountain of light. Thus was christened the world's most famous diamond!

After Nadir Shah's death, the Kohinoor passed into the hands of Ahmad Shah, the founder of

The British crown with the Kohinoor

the Durrani Dynasty. In 1813, Maharaja Ranjit Singh paid Rs 1.25 lakhs and bought the precious diamond from Shah Shuja, a descendant of Ahmad Shah Durrani. Thus, after a brief sojourn in Persia the diamond came back to India. When Punjab was annexed by the British East India Company at the end of a bloody battle in 1849, the diamond was formally handed over to the new Board of Governors. The Board decided to gift the precious stone to the Queen of England. The Kohinoor embarked on its final journey to London as a souvenir befitting the Queen who had it resized to fit the crown of her daughter, Princess Alexandra. Over the years, it was constantly reshaped till it was reduced to nearly one hundred and eight carats and set into the crown of Queen Elizabeth II. It is here that it remains encased even today as the pride and beauty of the British crown. It resides in the Tower of London among the crown jewels of the House of Windsor.

Legend has it that all men who possessed the famed Kohinoor, met with ill fate – be it Shahjahan, Aurungzeb or Nadir Shah. The queen was convinced that the stone would auger bad luck and decreed that it be adorned only by women.

The other important diamonds mined in Golconda include the Pitt or Regent diamond, weighing four hundred and ten carats when discovered in the eighteenth century by a slave near Golconda. The stone was owned by William Pitt, the English Prime Minister who sold it to the Duke of Orleans, the Regent of France. Louis XV wore it at his coronation and it also adorned the hat of Marie Antoinette. After the French Revolution it passed into the hands of Napolean Bonaparte who had it set in the hilt of his sword. It is now displayed in the Louvre Museum in Paris. The Nizam diamond weighing two hundred and seventy seven carats, the Great Table Diamond – a two hundred and forty two carat beauty and the Hope diamond weighing forty four carats were the other remarkable stones found here, but none of these are in India today. The Hope Diamond was considered to be cursed, as many of its owners died miserable deaths. Once owned by Louis XIV, it is now on display at the Smithsonian in Washington DC.

Once Brazil stumbled upon its diamond mines and diamonds were discovered in Africa, the Indian mines petered out. Other than diamonds, precious stones like garnet, amethyst, topaz, agate etc were also mined in the kingdom. Though the merchants traded in pearls, they were all imported from Persia.

The Kohinoor

AN ICON OF COMPOSITE CULTURE

Royal procession on elephants. Golconda c1680

Hyderabad, during the Qutub Shahi regime, was the nerve center of different cultures, art and traditions that gradually evolved into the renowned *Hyderabadi* way of life. The paintings and other art forms of the time reflect the opulent lifestyle of the rulers and the nobility. Exciting accounts of life within the fortress are said to have inspired many a fable, the most significant being the enduring tale of the 'Arabian Nights'. Evenings at Golconda were magical. The king and his nobles sipped wine or consumed opium as they enjoyed the music and dance performed by beautiful courtesans. Polo and *Kabaddi* were the popular sports.

Deccani painting and decorative art was ardently patronized by the Qutub Shahi rulers. The art form that flourished in this period was popularly known as the *Dakhani Qalam*. The earlier paintings depict a very Persian sensibility while the later works reveal a more *Dakhani* or the ethnic essence. Just like Mughal art, Deccan paintings were a blend of Persian, European and local influences. Since the Golconda kings had strong cultural links with Persia, most men and women depicted in the paintings were shown dressed in Persian costumes.

Horse and man. Golconda c1650

Madonna and child. Golconda c1675

The paintings of the 17th century were usually embellished with gold and characterized by the use of brilliant colours. Portraits of the women of the royal family reveal fine details of their attire, jewellery, and stately demeanour. The Golconda elite had a great fondness for flora as can be seen from the paintings of the era in which flowers and floral motifs figured prominently. Another favourite motif are birds which appear in unlikely places and were depicted in a style totally different from the Mughal paintings.

The art of fabric painting too, was explored by the Qutub Shahi artists and the scroll paintings on cloth were the largest examples of this art. Exquisite pieces of embroidery and *Pichchwais* of this period are to be found in both private and public collections the world over.

Calligraphy was patronized in this kingdom and was done not just on paper but also on stone. *Kalamkari* was another style that evolved in Golconda. *Kalamkari* as the name suggests was executed by *Kalam* or a pen using natural dyes and colours and was used for both religious and decorative ornamentation. It was in and around Machlipatnam that *Kalamkari* evolved. The *Kalamkari* paintings of Srikalahasti depicted imagery from the Hindu mythology and were used as temple hangings. Both human and animal forms along with floral patterns were meticulously illustrated in this art form. The commonly depicted figures were two peacocks facing each other or a dancing peacock and a tiger.

Ibrahim Quli Qutub Shah who had spent his early years in Vijaynagar was very fond of poets,

A Kalamkari painting depicting Krishna's Geeta Upadesh

singers and musicians and eminent Telugu poets like Addanki Gangadhar Kavi, Kundukura Rudra Kavi and Ponnaganti Teleganarya Kavi graced his court. The *Yayati Charitra* written by Ponniganti Teleganarya was dedicated to Amin Khan, a general of Ibrahim Quli Qutub Shah. Addanki Aangadharudu wrote *Tapati Samvaranopakhyanam* and dedicated it to the king. Kancharla Gopanna or Bhakta Ramdas wrote *Dasaradhi Satakam* and his *kirtans* or devotional songs in praise of Lord Rama were significant literary works of the time.

The king was a great connoisseur of music and dance and both were an essential part of celebrations, especially during festivals like Basant, Mirag-ki-Id or Navroz. Golconda celebrated the festival of Basant to welcome spring with a lot of colour and gaiety. Kuchipudi, the popular dance form of Andhra Pradesh survived during the medieval times due to the support of the Qutubshahi rulers. In 1678, on his way to Masulipatnam, Abdul Hasan Tana Shah stopped at the village of Kuchipudi and was so impressed by the performance of some young boys near the village temple, that he gifted the village to a few native Brahmin families devoted to this dance form.

Hyderabad, during the Qutub Shah era, exemplified a fusion of diverse cultures and traditions making it truly unique. During this time, it was a prominent town of southern India and along with cities like Agra, Delhi, Lahore, Ahmedabad, Multan, Dacca and Patna, emerged as an important center of economic and cultural progress.

Noted Kuchipudi dancer Ms Deepika Reddy

Hyderabad's growth was spectacular in terms of area, population, and economic activity as a large number of immigrants came and settled down here attracted by its moderate weather, hospitable people and promising prospects. The strategic location of the city helped it emerge as a major trading center of the east as not only local traders, but merchants from Persia and the Gulf were encouraged to come and trade here. The port of Masulipatnam was close by and the city was well linked to the other business towns like Surat, Goa, Bijapur and the Malabar Coast. European merchants had set up factories along the coast up to the port town of Masulipatnam.

The *Dakhani* culture was a beautiful amalgamation of Persian and Telugu traditions. Sultan Muhammad Quli's famous work, the *Kulliyat*, gives an authentic account of the social life and customs of the time. Scholars, thinkers and poets were patronized in the court irrespective of their caste, conviction or religion. All languages, be it Arabic, Persian, Telugu, Urdu or Marathi were evenly endorsed and encouraged by the King and the nobility. Muhammad Quli was an accomplished poet fluent even in Telugu and Telugu along with Persian was used for issuing the royal *farmans*. Harmony and camaraderie prevailed as the Hindus enthusiastically participated in the Muharram procession, imbibed interesting Islamic themes and stories and rendered them in Telugu folklore. Similarly, Hindu customs and wedding rituals were gladly adopted by the Muslims. The administration never stopped the construction of Hindu temples or interfered with their religious gatherings and even trusted Hindu personnel with important ranks in both civil and military administration. Akkanna and Madanna were the two important ministers during the regime of the last ruler of Golconda, Abul Hasan Tana Shah.

Dakhani was a blend of Persian, Arabic, Telugu, Hindi and Urdu. Charming and endearing, the language was the Qutub Shahi gift to Hyderabad. Muhammad Quli was a great patron of the language and promoted and enriched it. Persian *Ghazals* and poetry were translated into *Dakhani* and so were some Sanskrit works given a *Dakhani* rendition.

Rich traditions established then, grew stronger with time, giving the city an incredible legacy of vibrant customs, exciting rituals and a rich composite heritage.

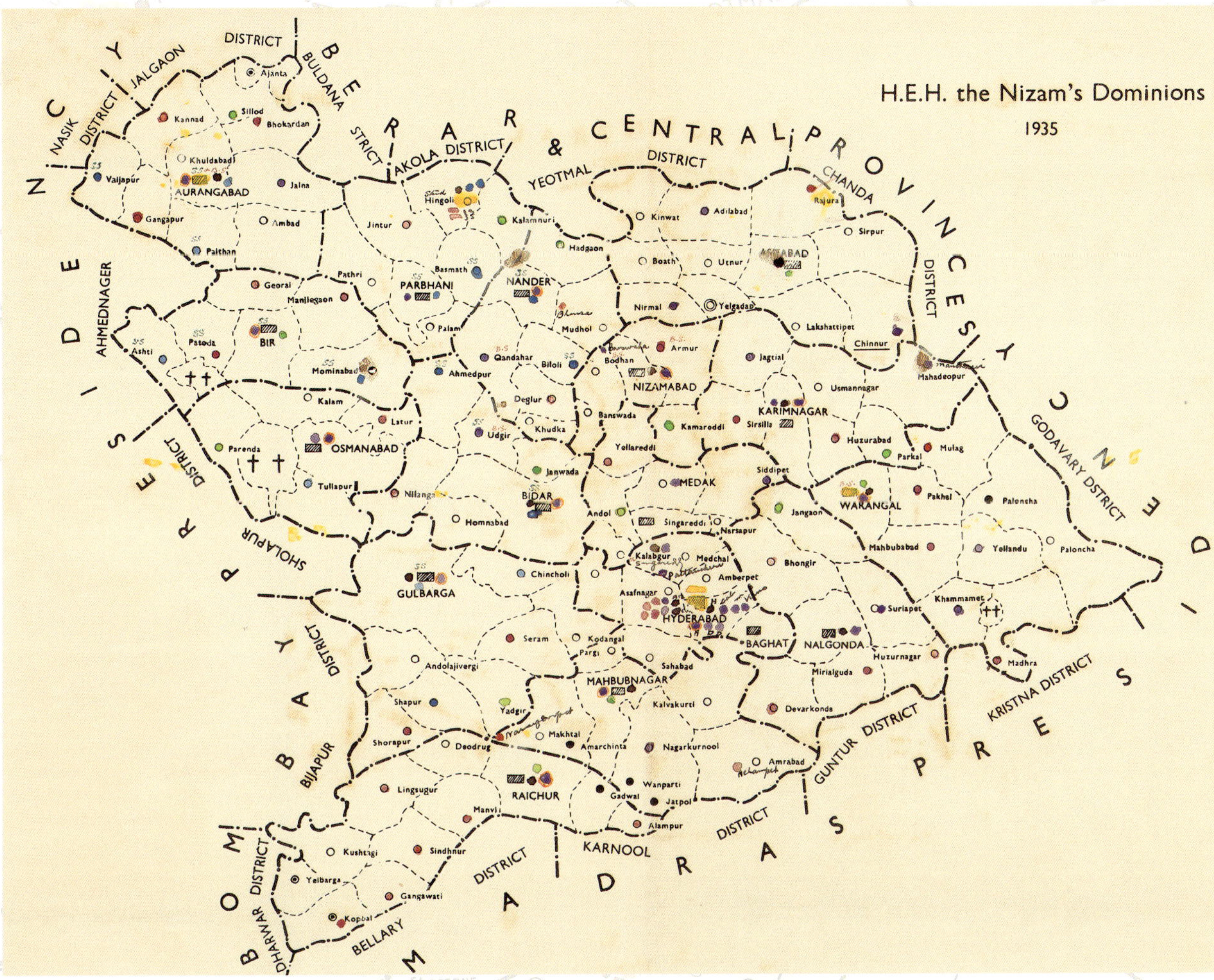
H.E.H. the Nizam's Dominions
1935
BERAR
CENTRAL PROVINCES
BOMBAY PRESIDENCY
MADRAS PRESIDENCY
AURANGABAD
PARBHANI
NANDER
ADILABAD
BIR
OSMANABAD
NIZAMABAD
KARIMNAGAR
BIDAR
MEDAK
WARANGAL
GULBARGA
HYDERABAD
BAGHAT
NALGONDA
MAHBUBNAGAR
RAICHUR
NASIK
JALGAON DISTRICT
BULDANA
AKOLA DISTRICT
YEOTMAL
CHANDA DISTRICT
GODAVARY DISTRICT
KRISTNA DISTRICT
GUNTUR DISTRICT
KARNOOL DISTRICT
BELLARY
DHARWAR DISTRICT
BIJAPUR DISTRICT
SHOLAPUR DISTRICT
AHMEDNAGER

In 1687 Golconda was seized by the Mughals and Deccan was ruled by the Mughal governors from Aurangabad. In 1713, the Mughal Emperor, Farruksiyar, appointed a twenty six year old warrior Qamruddin as the new Governor of Deccan. Qamruddin was the grandson of Chin Qilij Khan, Aurungzeb's brave commander who lost his life during the siege of Golconda. The young Governor proved to be an able administrator and earned the title of Nizam-ul-Mulk or the Governor of the Kingdom.

The next Mughal Emperor Mohammad Shah, impressed with the diligence and sincerity of Nizam-ul-Mulk appointed him the Prime Minister of the Mughal Empire. Though this was a great elevation for Nizam-ul-Mulk, he could not fit into blasé Delhi society and preferred to return to Aurangabad. On his way he met his old spiritual teacher Hazrat Nizamuddin Aurungabadi who offered him a plate full of *kulchas* (bread). Nizam-ul-Mulk was hungry and devoured seven of them. The holy man made a divine prediction – 'Since you ate seven *kulchas*, your dynasty would rule for seven generations!'

Nizam-ul-Mulk Asif Jah 1
(1724 – 1748)

In October 1724, Nizam-ul-Mulk declared himself *Subedar* or Governor of the six Deccan provinces – Aurangabad, Bidar, Bijapur, Berar, Adilabad and Hyderabad. His domain extended from the west to the east coast of southern India. Nizam-ul-Mulk was conferred the title of Asif Jah by the Mughal Emperor. It became the name of the new dynasty and his successors were called the Nizams. The new ruler chose a flag with a picture of a *kulcha* or bread against a field of yellow. The words *Azmat-au-Lillah* (Glory belongs only to God) were inscribed above the *kulcha* with the Nizam's name below it.

Nizam-ul-Mulk reorganized the administrative machinery, improved the finances, waged wars and concluded treaties independent of the Mughal Emperor as he enjoyed his complete trust. A lover of peace, he was forced to fight eighty seven battles during his lifetime. He maintained distant and nonaligned relations both with the British and the French. He was wise enough to realize the futility and potential danger involved in indulging either of these foreign powers. He negotiated peace when the Mughals were fighting a losing battle against Nadir Shah, the Persian invader on a rampage. He established his authority in the Deccan and his successors went on to rule for more than two centuries. Nizam-ul-Mulk laid the foundation of one of the most prosperous and renowned dynasties ever to have ruled the Deccan.

Nizam Ali Khan Asif Jah II
(1762 – 1803)

Nizam-ul-Mulk was survived by six sons and after his death a war of succession ensued between his sons and a grandson, Muzaffar Jung. In this phase of political instability, both the British and the French began to take advantage of the situation by pitting one sibling against the other. Around this time, the kingdom was attacked by the Marathas. Muzaffar Jung was killed and in 1751 and the French under Commander Bussy, installed Salabat Jung as the *Subedar* of Deccan. Between 1751 and 1762, the power of the French had eroded and the British slowly tightened their grip over the affairs of the state. Finally in 1762, the Mughal Emperor Shah Alam II appointed Nizam Ali Khan, the fourth son of Nizam-ul-Mulk, as the *Subedar* (Governor) of Deccan and conferred the title of Nizam-ul-Mulk, Asif Jah II on him.

At the age of twenty eight, Nizam Ali Khan, the fourth son of Nizam-ul-Mulk, became Governor and ruled the Deccan for forty two years. His reign was politically significant as this was the time when the Asif Jahi regime consolidated itself and also witnessed British ascendance.

A significant development of Nizam Ali Khan's reign was the shifting of the capital to Hyderabad on the ground that Auraungabad was close to the Maratha domain and thus susceptible to their repeated attacks. Once the capital moved to Hyderabad, the city saw tremendous economic and cultural growth. Nizam Ali Khan attacked the Marathas, defeated them and recovered the forts of Daulatabad, Sannrai, Asirgarh and Ahmednagar. But although he was triumphant, the hostility between the two powers never ceased. He also moved into the Chowmahalla palace which was home to nearly all his successors.

In 1766, the Nizam signed a treaty with the British whereby, in return for the Northern Circars, the British agreed to furnish the Nizam with a subsidiary force as and when required, or pay Rs 9 lakh per annum when the troops were not needed. The Nizam on his part committed to assist the British with his army. Trouble was brewing in Mysore where Hyder Ali, the Sultan of Mysore who coveted the area of modern day Karnataka, realized, that he needed to forge an alliance with the Nizam, isolate and defeat the British and repel the incessant Maratha attacks once and for all. The task was formidable but Hyder Ali pursued relentlessly. By 1767, he had vanquished the Marathas and sent a diplomatic mission to the Nizam headed by his young son Tipu Sultan. The Nizam agreed not to aid the British in the future. Soon after the First Mysore War broke out and the British, deprived of military support from the Nizam, were forced to accept the terms of peace dictated by Hyder Ali.

In 1780 the Second Mysore War started . Hyder Ali died and his son Tipu Sultan ascended the throne. Tipu tried in vain to convince the Nizam that their common enemy should be the British and not a fellow Muslim, but the Nizam went back to assisting the British. Realizing that it was impossible to match the British might, Tipu requested for a peace pact. In 1784, a treaty was signed but the settlement was short-lived.

In 1790, Lord Cornwallis, the new Governor General, deleted Tipu's name from the company's list of allies. An incensed Tipu retaliated with the Third Mysore War. The Nizam, accompanied by the British captain John Kennaway, led his army against Tipu. In 1792 Tipu was cornered and forced to sign another peace treaty. Tipu was not the only trouble maker for the Nizam. The Marathas too persisted with their attacks and in 1795 Nizam Ali Khan was forced to lead a mammoth army of ninety six thousand cavalry, forty four thousand infantry and one hundred and eight guns against the Marathas. He was ably assisted by a French general, Monsieur Raymond. The Nizam's army could not match the tenacity of the Marathas and was forced to cede the forts of Daulatabad, Ahmednagar and Sholapur and also concede a huge war indemnity.

By then problems began to mount in Hyderabad and the Nizam was forced to turn his attention to matters at home. His own eldest son, Prince Ali Jah, joined hands with Sadasiva Reddy, a Hindu chieftain of Medak, to depose him and usurp the throne. The Nizam sought military assistance from the British Resident, Captain William Kirkpatrick to crush the revolt. Sadasiva Reddy surrendered and was imprisoned while the prince committed suicide to escape his father's wrath.

In 1798, alarmed by the deteriorating discipline in his army and persuaded by his own nobles, the Nizam signed the Subsidiary Alliance with the

British. He realized that the British troops would be useful against the nagging Maratha aggression on one hand and Tipu Sultan of Mysore on the other. Lord Wellesley, the new Governor General, instructed the British Resident, Kirkpatrick, to negotiate the terms of the settlement. According to the terms of the treaty, the British agreed to station six battalions in Hyderabad for which the Nizam would pay them a handsome sum. The French contingent in the Nizam's army was to be disbanded immediately. Fourteen thousand French troops and one hundred and twenty four officers left Hyderabad and the legendary Corps Francois De Raymond became history. The clever manipulation of the British led to the complete disarmament of the Nizam's French force.

The most significant development of this time was the stationing of the British troops near Bolarum. The British cantonment established in 1798 stayed on for the next century and a half.

In 1803, after a long and arduous rule of 42 years, Nizam Ali Khan died. He was succeeded by Sikander Jah.

Saga of The French General Monsieur Raymond

While the reign of the second Nizam, Asif Jah II, witnessed the ascendancy of the British, there was one man who was determined to foil every British attempt to control Deccan. This was a French gentleman, Monsieur Michel Joachim Marie Raymond who dreamt of establishing French supremacy over Southern India by winning over the local rulers.

When Pondicherry was taken over by the British in 1778, Raymond fled to Mysore and joined hands with Hyder Ali. In 1786 Raymond joined the services of the Nizam as a captain in his army. He set up an ammunition factory where he made amazing cannons and muskets for the Nizam's army, in an area which was later named Gunfoundry. The Nizam grew very fond of him and on his orders Raymond headed a fifteen thousand strong army of soldiers. His own battalion of French troops called the Corps Francois de Raymond became an integral part of the Nizam's army. The Nizam showered him with praises and privileges much to the resentment of the British Resident, Kirkpatrick, who was working on a plan to win over the Nizam and ultimately control Deccan. Amidst all the adulation, the fear of the rising British influence haunted Raymond, as the Nizam had begun to associate increasingly with the British.

In March 1798, unable to handle his disappointment and frustration he shot his two dogs, his horse and finally himself. Another version holds that he was poisoned. He was buried next to an obelisk on a hilltop overlooking the French cantonment. Raymond's Hindu followers deified him as Musa Ram or son of Moses, while his Muslim supporters worshipped him as Musa Rahim.

British are here to stay

At the end of the seven years war, both the English and the French reiterated the belief of the former French governor Dupliex, that India had to be controlled by the Europeans. After failing to capture Madras, losing Pondicherry in a British counter-attack and forced out of

Hyderabad, the French had lost the game. The British, however, had shrewdly strengthened their base in the southern part of the country. In 1779, Mr Holland was sent as a diplomat to the Nizam's court. He settled down at Bolarum, a small village to the north of Hyderabad and thus was established the institution of the British Residents, accountable only to the Governor General of India, ostensibly to gain the Nizam's goodwill and friendship but actually to keep a watchful eye on the Nizam and his political manoeuvres. This institution stayed on in Hyderabad till 1947 when the British finally moved out of India.

At the end of the fourth Mysore war in 1799, Tipu Sultan was killed and the British had come one step closer to establishing their supremacy in the south. Wellesely handed over the kingdom of Mysore to a five year old descendant of the ruling Hindu family. Most of the wealth of the kingdom was shared by the Nizam of Hyderabad and the British East India Company.

Though the Nizam was relieved of the burden of any further aggression from Mysore, he had unwittingly invited bigger trouble by joining hands with the British. Little did he realize that the establishment of a permanent cantonment on the outskirts of the city was a part of a larger game plan which would result in his being reduced to a puppet in the hands of the British.

Jawans training at the EME center, Secunderabad

Lashkar – where Winston Churchill lived

To the north of the city in the British Cantonment, an East India Company Force under Colonel Lang made permanent residence. The Nizam's personal army too was stationed here and the entire area was called Lashkar. Gradually, a parade ground, a polo ground, race course, cricket, football and hockey fields too came up around here. In the 1870's a young subaltern was posted here. He lived and trained at Lashkar and spent his spare time playing polo and golf. The bungalow where he lived named 'The Retreat', still stands, and curious onlookers stop to admire the building that was once the home of none other than England's greatest Prime Minister – Sir Winston Churchill.

Today, the twin cities of Secunderabad and Hyderabad have one of the biggest cantonments in the country. The major institutions located within the cantonment are the Electrical and Mechanical Engineers Center, the Army Ordnance Corps Center and the Armed Forces Dental Medical College at Bolarum, a Military College of Electronics & Mechanical Engineering at Trimulgherry and an Artillery Centre at Mehdipatnam. The nation's premier Airforce Academy is located in Dundigal along with the two Airforce Stations at Hakimpet and Begumpet.

The house where Churchill lived

James Kirkpatrick and his romance with Khairunissa.

Many British Residents came and went, but the most flamboyant of the lot was the sixth Resident, James Achilles Kirkpatrick. James Kirkpatrick was a handsome Scotsman who succeeded his own brother William Kirkpatrick. To the young Resident could be attributed the most critical negotiations and treaties signed between the British and the Hyderabad state during the time of the second Nizam. The Nizam was very fond of him and treated him like his son. The feelings were mutual. The Resident in a letter dated 1801 referred to the Nizam endearingly as 'my father of adoption-old Nizzy!'

The young Resident was very popular in the social milieu, entertaining in style and being entertained as well by the Nizam and the nobility. A romance brewed in Hyderabad which in the years to come, became the theme of many romantic plays and novels. A beautiful young Muslim girl, Khairunissa, saw the handsome young Resident when he was riding home one day. Led by her mother and grandmother, Khair decided to meet the Resident. When she expressed her desire to befriend him, the Resident was taken aback. Khairunissa was in a hurry because she was engaged to an old Nawab whom she didn't want to marry. James too fell in love with her and sought the Nizam's permission to marry the fourteen year old Khair. The Nizam agreed but the girl's grandfather, a powerful noble and *Bakshi* or the paymaster in the Nizam's court, objected to the wedding. This unusual love affair became a reason for great public outrage in the orthodox Muslim society of Hyderabad. When Lord Wellesley heard of the romantic dalliance of his Resident, he was upset, but did not stop the Resident from marrying Khairunissa.

With the blessings of the Nizam, James Kirkpatrick and Khairunissa Begum became man and wife. Khairunissa gave birth to a son and a daughter, but in 1803 Kirkpatrick sent his two infant children to England to be brought up under foster care. Khairunissa was heartbroken. By 1805, Colonel Kirkpatrick was not keeping good health and proceeded to Calcutta to recuperate and also confer with the Governor General about the political developments in Hyderabad. He could not recover from his illness and died in Calcutta. Khairunissa died later but how and when is not known.

Khairunissa

Sikander Jah, Asif Jah III
(1803 – 1829)

Sikander Jah, the son of Nizam Ali Khan took over in 1803, ably assisted by the proficient statesman Mir Alam, the new Prime Minister of Hyderabad.

Secunderabad the birth of the twin city

Around this time, to the north of the old town, the new city of Secunderabad came up. Named after the new Nizam, the city grew around the British garrison which later became one of the largest British cantonments in India. Secunderabad boasted of bazaars, schools, a church, hospital and a new residential area. It witnessed a significant influx as more and more people moved in, to escape the chaotic conditions in the old city. Between the 3rd and 11th of June 2006, Secunderabad celebrated two hundred years of its existence with great fanfare.

The Palmer Scandal

The infamous Palmer scandal was a blot on Sikander Jah's reign. William Palmer was the head of the banking house, William Palmer and company that managed the Nizam's finances. After the demise of Prime Minister Mir Alam, his son Munir-ul-Mulk took over. He led an extravagant lifestyle and along with Chandulal, the new *Peshkar* borrowed excessively from the bank, in theory to pay the salary of the British soldiers in the Nizam's army.

Sir Charles Metcalfe, the new Resident was alarmed at the government's mounting debt and also noticed that most of the monthly payments instead of reaching the treasury, were being diverted to Palmer and Company as a negotiating bonus. Hyderabad stood on the brink of bankruptcy. Lord Hastings, the Governor General of the East India Company, Lord Hastings, took matters in his hand and arbitrated a settlement by which he paid ten million rupees from the company's financial credit to settle Palmer and Company's dues and saved the Nizam from imminent insolvency. By doling out this largesse he won over the Nizam completely.

At age sixty one, Sikander Jah passed away. Before his death, he advised his son and heir,

Nasir-ud-Daula, to continue the amicable relationship with the British for he knew well where the real power rested.

Nasir-ud-Daula Asif Jah IV
(1829 – 1857)

In 1829, the eldest son of Sikander Jah, Nawab Nasir-ud-Daula succeeded his father. His reign ushered in several reforms that rooted out corruption, mal-administration and financial disorder that were gnawing away at the administrative structure.

Social issues like *Sati*, selling of children, child marriages, failing educational system, recruitment of outsiders instead of Hyderabadis for local jobs and local resentment towards preference to Urdu over Telugu as the official language, plagued the government. In 1848, on the recommendation of his minister Nawab Siraj-ul-Mulk, the Nizam promulgated a law that prohibited '*Sati*' or the practice of immolation of the Hindu widow on her husband's pyre. The custom of selling children was banned in 1856.

In 1853, the Nizam signed a new treaty by which he agreed to cede Berar and other bordering districts up to Sholapur that would yield an annual income of over 5 million to the British who in return would maintain an auxiliary force for the Nizam. The Berar treaty strained the relations between the British and the Nizam for almost a century to come.

Another highlight of the fourth Nizam's reign was the appointment of Salar Jung I a young twenty four year old noble, as the Prime Minister of the state. The young and erudite Salar Jung took over at a critical juncture when the relations with the British were not congenial nor was the state's finance in order. The young man proved to be a capable administrator who went on to serve three Nizams and helped introduce both financial and administrative reforms to restore the sagging administrative framework .

The entire dominion was divided into sixteen districts and each placed under a *Taluqdar* (Magistrate) who was entrusted with the civil and judicial administration of the district. Records of land under cultivation were to be prepared annually with details like the nature of the crop, name of the land owner and the tax due to the government. The farmer was given the concession of making part payment of his land dues when his crop failed. These measures went a long way in creating an accountable system of revenue collection and land reforms. The Chaderghat Bridge was built during this time.

After ruling for twenty eight years, Nawab Nasir-ud-Daula passed away and the new Nizam was his eldest son Nawab Afzal-ud-Daula.

Afzal-ud-Daula, Asif Jah V
(1857 – 1869)

Nawab Afzal-ud-Daula's coronation coincided with the outbreak of India's First War of Independence when northern India was up in flames. In Hyderabad too, the Rohillas attacked the British Residency, but it was firmly repelled by the able Prime Minister, Salar Jung I. A similar uprising in Sholapur could not be contained by the king there and Sholapur and Raichur were handed over to the Nizam after the suppression of the mutiny. These two territories yielded a revenue of 2.1 million to the Nizam.

Afzal-ud-Daula, Asif Jah V

After the Mutiny of 1857, the mighty Mughal Empire disintegrated. The Nizam at the behest of the British, ordered for the immediate removal of the Mughal Emperor, Bahadur Shah Zafar's name from the coins and also discontinued the practice of including the Mughal Emperor's name in the Friday prayers.

During the reign of the fifth Nizam, the state was divided into five *Subas* (divisions) and sixteen districts. Each *Suba* was headed by a *Subedar* and each district was placed under a *Taluqdar*. A new rail line called the Nizam's Guaranteed Railway was introduced to connect Hyderabad to the Bombay-Madras line. The rail link helped promote the economic growth of the state. In 1855, a Central Treasury was established and in 1856 the Stamp Paper Office was set up. All shops selling liquor were shut down. The Afzalgunj Mosque, the Afzal Gunj Bridge and the Afzal Gunj Bazaar were all built during Afzal-ud-Daula's reign. Pleased with his loyalty during the troubled year of the Mutiny, Queen Victoria conferred the title of G.C.S.I or the Order of the Star of India on the Nizam.

Unfortunately, the Nizam passed away at a young age of forty two, after a peaceful reign of twelve years. The heir apparent was his three year old son Nawab Mir Mahboob Ali Khan.

Mir Mahboob Ali Khan

Asif Jah VI (1869 – 1911)

Mir Mahboob Ali Khan was born in 1866 and was just two years and seven months old when he lost his father. The infant was coronated on the insistence of Salar Jung I, Shams-ul-Umara and the Resident. Salar Jung and Nawab Shams-ul-Umara were to be the co-regents who would run the administration on behalf of the young Nizam.

Mir Mahboob Ali Khan

After the death of Shams-ul Umara, Sir Salar Jung took upon himself the task of grooming the young Nizam. In 1883, Sir Salar Jung died and a provisional council of Regency with Mahboob Ali Khan as the President and Mir Laiq Ali Khan, son of Sir Salar Jung I as secretary, was constituted to supervise the affairs of the state. In 1885, the young Nizam was invested with full administrative powers by Lord Rippon, the then Governor General of India. In 1883 Mir Laiq Ali Khan was given the title of Salar Jung II and was later appointed the Prime Minister of Hyderabad. Salar Jung II promised to continue the pace of reforms set in motion by his father but in 1887, he was forced to resign due to court intrigues. The Nizam now took full control over the administration and was ably assisted by Sir Asman Jah, the new Prime Minister. In 1893, after serving the Nizam for six years, Sir Asman Jah resigned and Sir Viqar-ul-Umara was appointed the Prime Minister. In 1902 Sir Viqar-ul Umara passed away and Maharaja Kishen Pershad, a Hindu noble was appointed the Prime Minister of Hyderabad.

In 1902, a treaty was signed with the British and the district of Berar was handed over to the British on a permanent lease, for a payment of twenty five lakh rupees per annum. The Nizam's dejure sovereignty was recognized over Berar and the Asif Jahi flag was allowed to be hoisted on Nizam's birthdays. The Hyderabad contingent was disbanded and became a part of the British army.

A young Mahboob Ali Khan

A large number of administrative reforms were introduced during the time of the sixth Nizam to improve Hyderabad's socio-economic state. A new rail line was introduced, cotton mills were opened at Hyderabad, Gulbarga and Aurangabad, new irrigation policies were initiated and old tanks were repaired. In 1893, through a proclamation called the '*Qanunche Mubarik*' Mahboob Ali Pasha introduced a Cabinet Council to oversee the administrative matters and a Legislative Council to create a legal framework for the state. The government departments of Police, Judiciary, Excise and Forest were revamped.

Education was a subject close to the Nizam's heart and he was keen to introduce reforms in this sector too. As a result, in 1878, the *Madarsa-i-Aliya* was founded and in 1908 Mahboobia Girl's school was established. In 1891, the Asifia State Library was setup to conserve rare Arabic and Persian books and manuscripts. Medical facilities and medical education were given special attention. In 1887, the prestigious Nizam College was established with Dr. Aghorenath Chattopadhyay as the Principal.

On the 5th of February 1885, the British Queen conferred the honour of the Grand Commander of the Star of India on Mahboob Ali Pasha. In 1911, at the age of forty six, Mahboob Ali Pasha breathed his last. He was succeeded by his son, Mir Osman Ali Khan, who would be the seventh and the last Nizam of Hyderabad.

Mir Mahboob Ali Khan – the Beloved Prince

Mir Mahboob Ali Khan popularly known as Mahboob Ali Pasha, was the most admired of all the Nizams. Mahboob in Urdu means beloved and the sixth Nizam was indeed loved by his subjects. Large hearted and compassionate, he governed more with his heart and *Hyderabadis* love to regale visitors with vignettes from the life of their beloved prince.

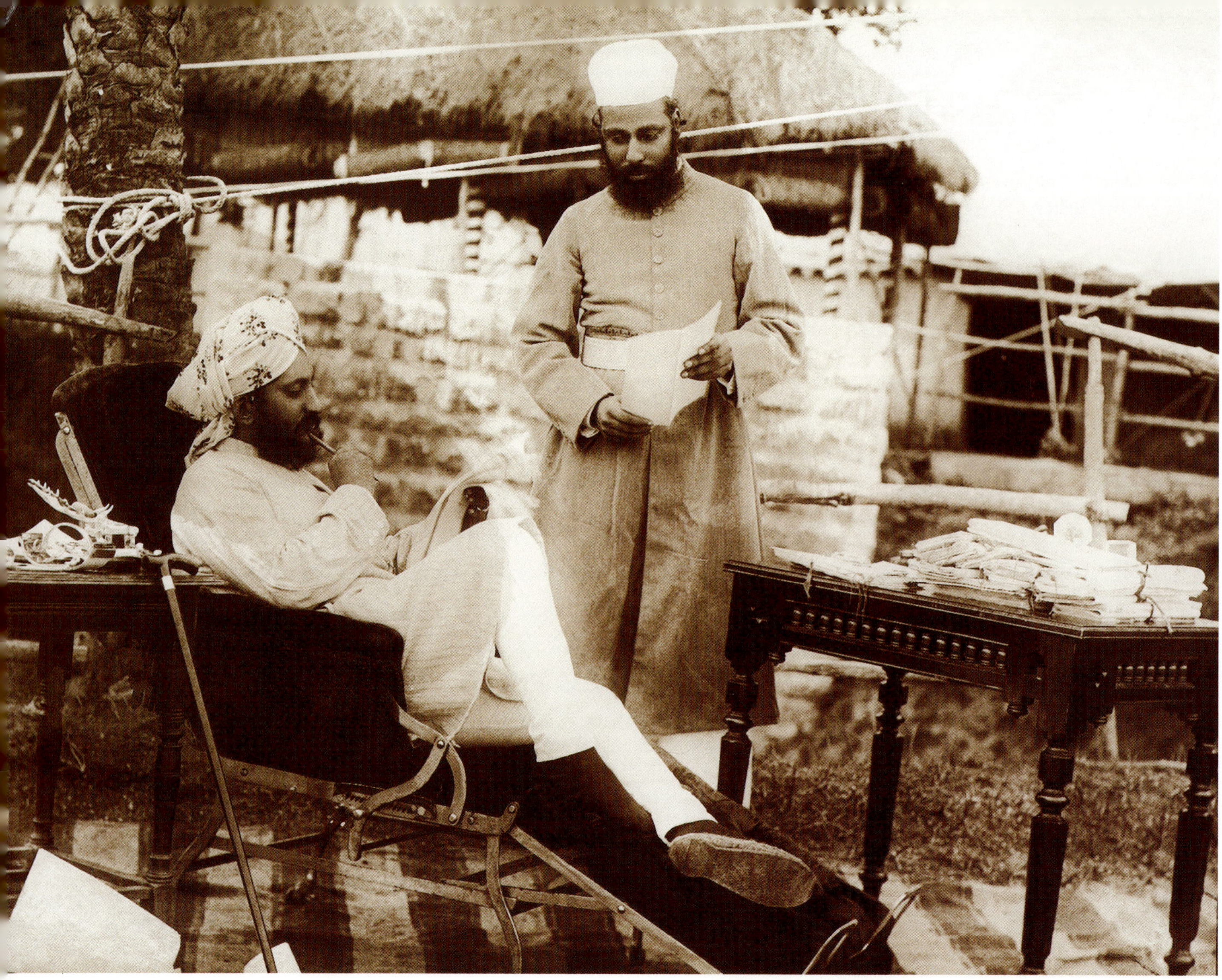

The tale of the Chandeliers

Mahboob Ali Pasha as we all know, was coronated when he was barely two years old. Salar Jung I, who was the Prime Minister of the state, was appointed his guardian and mentor. One day, the playful prince broke an expensive chandelier in the hallway. The prince was frightened at the loud noise it made, and so were all the palace staff. A little later, the Prime Minister walked in. There was a deafening silence. 'Did you do this?' asked the old man sternly. The scared prince nodded without saying a word. 'I cannot tolerate such behaviour from the future Nizam of Hyderabad. Bring me my walking stick,' ordered the Prime Minister. He then asked the prince to show him his right hand. The young boy offered his trembling hand. Salar Jung thrust his walking stick into the

Mahboob Ali Khan loved hunting

young prince's hand. 'You are the Nizam of Hyderabad. This palace belongs to you and so does everything in it,' said the minister firmly. 'Now step forward and break every chandelier in this palace.'

The gleeful young prince followed his orders and broke every chandelier that he could reach. Such was the confidence instilled in the young prince by Salar Jung who remained the greatest influence in Mahboob Ali Khan's life.

A fortunate woman

Very often, Mahboob Ali Pasha would walk the streets, incognito, to get to know the condition of his people. On one such tour, he saw an old woman carrying a lunch box and rushing towards the Purani Haveli, the Nizam's splendid palace. The shabbily dressed Nizam stopped the lady and asked her where she was going. The old woman was visibly annoyed at being interrupted by a stranger and said that she was carrying lunch for her son who was a guard at the Nizam's palace. The disguised Nizam said he too, was hungry and asked for something to eat. The old woman offered the scruffy old man some food from the lunch box. The old man ate something, thanked the woman and disappeared in the crowd. When the lady reached the palace and opened the box she found that the lunch box was filled with gold coins. The stranger was none other than the Nizam himself!

The Blessed Farmer

There are many such tales - tales of a prince with a heart of gold. A poor farmer, whose daughter just got married, was in debt and wrote to the Nizam asking for five hundred rupees. The Nizam signed the letter ordering that the farmer be granted five thousand rupees. The secretary to the Nizam, on reading the note thought that the Nizam had misread the request and once again submitted the letter to the Nizam. This time the letter came back with 'one' added before the five and the total grant now amounting to fifteen thousand rupees. The secretary immediately understood the Nizam's

Commander in Chief Sir Afsar-ul-Mulk

intention and arranged for the grant. The lucky farmer couldn't believe his good fortune.

The impudent child

The Nizam once visited the home of his Commander-in-Chief, Sir Afsar-ul-Mulk. The impudent son of the commander was rude to the royal guest, much to the embarrassment of his father. The Nizam's reaction however shocked the commander. 'No one has ever dared to be discourteous to me', said the Nizam. 'This indeed is an incredible experience and I offer a pension of hundred pounds a year to your child.'

The lucky shopkeeper

When Mahboob Ali Pasha heard that the owner of a reputed store in the city was bankrupt, but was too proud to ask for help, he decided to visit the store. He stepped in and indicated to his lieutenant that he wanted to buy everything displayed there.

The Nizam turned around, stepped into his carriage and the '*baggi*' drove away. His servants paid for the entire merchandise and carried it to the palace.

The fortunate peasant

Tales of the Nizam's generosity had spread far and wide and a poor farmer walked into the Nizam's court seeking help. He had seven daughters but no money to get them married. The Nizam took out his purse and handed it over to the farmer. The poor peasant was thrilled and began counting the coins. 'Your Highness, the purse has only two hundred rupees. How is that going to help me?'
The Nizam replied, 'what can I do? It's your luck so deal with it.' Quick came the repartee. 'I am well acquainted with my luck. I came to benefit from yours.'

The Nizam was stumped by the clever reply. He ordered his minister to grant fourteen thousand rupees to the farmer.

A troublesome neighbour

Next to the Purani Haveli was the home of a noble, Shahab Jung who had a weird routine. He slept during the day and worked through the night. At night there would be a flurry of activity in his house while the days were absolutely quiet. Due to the noble's odd working hours, the Nizam had a tough time getting some sleep. His servants went up to the noble and complained. The harried noble rushed to the court and apologized profusely.

'I may be forgiven for disturbing the Nizam. I just have this one modest home whereas His Highness has so many magnificent palaces in the city. If His Highness chose to move to any of his other palaces, his nights would be totally peaceful.'

Instead of getting angry at the cheeky suggestion, the Nizam laughed and never complained again.

The raging river Musi and the floods of 1908

The Musi River would often get flooded destroying lives and property. In the autumn of 1908, the frenzied Musi rose an alarming twenty feet in six hours and raged through the city destroying buildings and bridges and killing more than fifteen thousand people. Nearly one fourth of the population was rendered homeless. Hyderabad was devastated!

The Nizam drove around the city in his new acquisition – a motor car, supervising relief operation, comforting his people and offering shelter, food and clothes to his distraught subjects. He opened the doors of his palaces for the homeless and distressed. So moved was the compassionate ruler that he even agreed to perform Hindu rituals to placate the irate river. On the suggestion of his Hindu nobles and priests, the Nizam took a gold tray loaded with special offering and rode to the riverside. He stepped into the water and offered the tray to the River Goddess. The tray was swept away and people say that from that very moment the river began to recede. The incident reflects the tolerance of the sixth Nizam towards all religion and people.

The defiant Nizam – An interesting encounter with the Governor General.

In 1903 a grand *Durbar* was held in Delhi in honour of King Edward VII, the King of England. Nizam Mahboob Ali Pasha attended the impressive *Durbar.* Lord Curzon, the British Governor General, announced that he desired to garland every Indian prince present in the gathering. The Nizam was the first in line. When the Governor General stepped forward to garland him, Mahboob Ali Pasha instead of bowing before him, drew his sword. Everyone was taken aback.

Flooded Musi, 1908

Mahboob Ali Khan, 1904

'My neck is here today, but maybe gone tomorrow. But this sword which was given to me by my father will be held by my son tomorrow and so on. Not my neck, but my sword is my mark of loyalty to you. Please garland the sword,' said the Nizam. The entire gathering was stunned. There was a moment of silence. Lord Curzon walked up to the prince and hung the garland around the sword.

The case in point proved that though the Nizam had accepted the British authority, he didn't allow the foreigners to subjugate his conscience.

Another show of defiance

Once, Mahboob Ali Pasha reached Delhi to attend a *Durbar*. The Nizam, head of the richest state in India made a strange request. He asked for an elephant to be brought to the platform to take him to the city. The Governor General was taken aback at the strange request and turned it down. The defiant Nizam in turn, refused to disembark from his railway carriage. He nonchalantly dined, played cards and enjoyed his siesta in his luxurious coach, unmindful of the chaos he was creating. Several trains carrying other rulers of princely states began to lineup behind the Nizam's. The desperate Governor General could do little to convince the defiant Nizam and was left with no choice but to send an elephant to the railway platform. Mahboob Ali Pasha had yet again had his way with the British. The pleased Nizam climbed onto the elephant carriage and rode into the city.

The famous wardrobe at Purani Haveli

Mir Mahboob Ali Khan had a penchant for good clothes and his wardrobe was so commodious and wide-ranging that a lot of his outfits had been worn only once. To accommodate his large collection of clothes, he had a two hundred and forty feet long wardrobe built at Purani Haveli. The wardrobe was on either side of the hallway

The wardrobe at Purani Haveli

and had one hundred and thirty three built in cupboards to accommodate his large collection of clothes, shoes, hats and accessories. A manually operated lift imported from London and installed at one end of the hall, brought the Nizam to his enormous wardrobe every day.

The whimsical Nizam

Mahboob Ali Pasha's fascination for well tailored suits was proverbial. He once summoned a renowned stylist from Calcutta to tailor his suits and ordered that the entire bale of the selected fabric be used up so that no one else could ever use it.

After a few months, the consignment of seventy stitched suits reached Hyderabad. By now the whimsical Nizam had lost interest in them and ordered that the dresses be given away to the nobles. There was a hitch though. Each box did not contain a complete outfit. While some had only shirts, others had trousers while still others contained jackets. The nobles exchanged and tried out the dresses until each had a complete outfit. However there was one unlucky *Jagirdar* who was stuck with seventy odd collars which he wore for the next thirty years!

The Nizam was a great horse lover and along with one of his favourite wives, Sardar Begum, avidly followed the races. He had a beautiful new home called Mahboob Mansion built for her overlooking the Malakpet Racecourse. As Muslim women could not be seen in public, she watched the races from behind a gold screen in her balcony.

The motor car ushers in the twentieth century

In 1905, the Prince and Princess of Wales visited Hyderabad. Motor cars were imported from England for the Prince's convoy. The Nizam was so fascinated by this new mode of transport that he ordered a few for himself. He now buzzed around town in his new acquisition much to the bewilderment of the *Hyderabadis* who had never seen such a contraption before.

European women on a bullock cart.

Peaceful coexistence.

A car showroom in Hyderabad

Mahboob Ali Khan with son Osman Ali Khan and visiting foreign dignitaries, 1905

Hunting and riding were his other hobbies. He was a sharp shooter and is said to have shot thirty tigers in his lifetime. The area beyond the old city was a thick jungle where the Nizam loved to hunt for leopards and the black buck.

In 1911, at Falaknuma, Mahboob Ali Pasha breathed his last.

Mir Osman Ali Khan

Asif Jah VII (1911 – 1948)

Mir Osman Ali Khan, the second child of Mahboob Ali Pasha, was born on April 6, 1886. He was proclaimed the Nizam of Hyderabad immediately after his father's death and the formal coronation took place on September 12, 1911. As a child, Osman Ali Khan was tutored by an English gentleman, Brian Edgerton, and lived next door to his mother whom the young prince was allowed to visit just once a week.

The seventh Nizam's reign was the most remarkable as it witnessed two World Wars, India's independence from the British and the merger of Hyderabad with the Union of India. Barely three years into Osman Ali Khan's regime, Europe was afire with the outbreak of the First World War. Nizam, a faithful ally of the British, offered them both military and financial assistance. The Hyderabad Imperial Service Cavalry was dispatched to Egypt to serve under the British Army. In 1918 he was conferred the title of 'His Exalted Highness' and later the 'Faithful Ally of the British Government'.

The Prince of Wales inspecting the guard of honour at Falaknuma, 1922

The highlight of Osman Ali Khan's reign was the establishment of Osmania University in 1917, with Urdu as the medium of instruction. It was the first time in India that a university offered an Indian language instead of English as a medium of instruction. Fourteen hundred acres of land were acquired for this purpose and the Nizam formally laid the foundation of the university in July, 1934. Built at a cost of 3.6 million, it is undoubtedly a remarkable legacy of the Nizam. *(Seen here is the insignia of Osmania University which is actually the first letter (ain) of Osman Ali Khan's name in Persian).* In 1927, Osmania Medical College and in 1929, Osmania Engineering College were established which till today are acclaimed institutes of academic excellence.

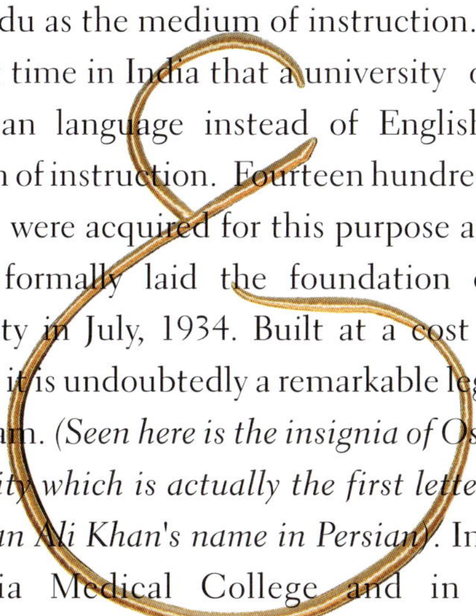

The city of Hyderabad was devastated by the frequent flooding of the Musi. In 1920, the Nizam ordered the construction of a dam across the river, ten kilometer upstream, aptly named the Osman Sagar. The dam was also meant to create a drinking water reservoir for the city of Hyderabad. In 1927 another reservoir, Himayat Sagar, designed by Sir Visweswaraiya was built to augment the water supply in the city and till date these two tanks continue to be the major reservoirs of Hyderabad. As a part of flood and river protection scheme, the preliminary work on Nagarjunasagar dam – a massive hydro electric project on the Krishna River, the Wyra project dam and the Paler Project dam were initiated. The Ali Sagar and Nizam Sagar – two major reservoirs and irrigation projects in Nizamabad were completed. Major industries like Shahabad Cement, Sirpur Paper Mills and the Nizam Sugar Factory were also set up during the reign of the seventh Nizam.

In 1919, the Nizam introduced the Executive Council to restructure and improve the functioning of the government and Sir Ali Imam was appointed its first President. The Executive Council's first significant job was the separation of the judiciary from the executive – a reform that the Indians had been demanding from the British and Hyderabad was the first to introduce.

In 1936, the British accepted the Nizam's nominal sovereignty over Berar and agreed to pay Berar's surplus revenue to the Nizam. However, the administration of Berar remained with the British. In 1923, a royal Durbar held at Chowmahalla Palace celebrated the completion of two hundred years of Asif Jahi rule. In 1936, the Silver Jubilee commemoration of Osman Ali Khan's reign was celebrated in grand style.

Mir Osman Ali Khan

In 1939, the Second World War broke out. The Nizam, a faithful ally of the British, went all out to help the British. Be it men, money or material, the Nizam stood like a rock behind the Allied army and Sir Winston Churchill in a letter acknowledged the service rendered by the Nizam. Hyderabad State spent over six crore and seventy one lakh rupees on the war.

In 1933, after more than a century, the Residency and the area around it was returned to the Nizam by the Resident Terence Keyes. In 1945, the southern part of Secunderabad was also handed over to the Nizam.

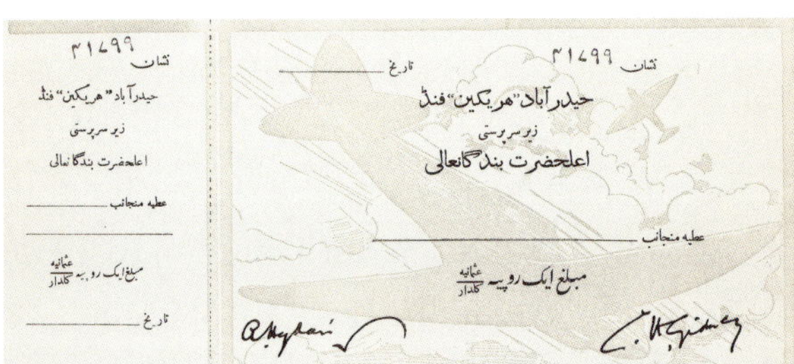

A raffle ticket issued to raise funds for the World War II

The Nizam State Railway

Hyderabad State had its own postal system, railways, roadways and airways under the State Department. The Nizam State Railway had the unique distinction of controlling not just the railway but the road and air services as well. During the reign of the seventh Nizam, the railway network was appreciably expanded to cover the entire state. By the 1940's, the rail network in the state spread over 2000 miles of broad and meter gauge lines. In 1940, elegantly furnished diesel rail cars were introduced for the convenience of the passengers.

Under the aegis of the Nizam's State Railway, buses were introduced for the city dwellers. It is believed that Mir Osman Ali Khan wanted to name the transport department after his mother, Begum Zehra, but the clerics advised him against it. However, the tradition of including the alphabet Z in the registration number of all state run public transport vehicles was established and still exists!

Hyderabad Railway Station

In 1938, an Air Department was created under the State Railway Administration. The department trained pilots and provided charter services and technical assistance to the State

Kachiguda Railway Station

A driving license issued during Osman Ali Khan's reign

A bus ticket of NSR

Buses of the Nizam State Railway

The Begumpet Airport inaugurated in 1932

Aero Club. In 1932, to facilitate air travel, a civil aviation board was formed and an aerodrome built at Begumpet. By the end of the Second World War, twenty one air companies had been setup in the country including Deccan Airways Limited set up in 1945. With time, Deccan Airways gained a reputation for being the most efficient airline in India.

The Air Force Station at Hakimpet

Much later, one early morning in 1951, the residents of Hakimpet village on the city outskirts, were rudely awakened by the noise of howling aircrafts. These were young pilots training on the Spitfire and Tempest on an airfield at Hakimpet which was in disuse since the Second World War. A Conversion Training Unit was established here, where fighter pilots were groomed to fly the Spitfire MK 1X and Tempest IIA trainers.

The unit grew rapidly and was renamed the Jet Training Wing in 1958, the Fighter Training Wing in 1968 and finally in 1983 evolved into the Airforce Station, Hakimpet. At this premier training station, young pilots honed their flying skills befitting the motto of the station which is

Squadron Leader Chandra and Flying Officer Sandeep Ranwa

Flying Officer Abhay Kumar Singh and
Flying Officer Dhiraj Ahlawat

Karmasu Kaushalam or 'Skill in Action'. In December 1995, history was rewritten, when for the first time, women pilots trained and passed out from the station.

From Spitfire and Tempest to Iskra and Kiran; from the Chinese to the Pakistan War - for the pilots at Hakimpet, the flight has been long but exhilarating!

Osman Ali Khan with Maulana Azad and Pandit Jawaharlal Nehru, 1951

The coming of the end

Hyderabad enjoyed the exalted status of being the largest of the three hundred and sixty two princely states in India. Any economic progress seemed impossible with Hyderabad's land locked geographical status and even for it to stay independent, an access to the sea was essential. In 1945 when the British agreed to return the southern part of the Secunderabad cantonment to the Nizam, he requested the restoration of the Northern Circars as that would provide Hyderabad with an entry into the sea.

On the 10th of July 1947, the 'Declaration of the Indian Independence' bill was introduced by Harold Macmillan. To the Nizam's dismay, no mention or decision was taken regarding the state of Hyderabad. Osman Ali Khan had a lurking fear that the partition of India was imminent and that the divide would be on communal lines. Since in Hyderabad, the two major communities, the Hindus and the Muslims had always lived in harmony, he saw no reason to support the partition. All princely states were given the option to either join India, Pakistan or remain independent. All states that would join the Indian Union would have to surrender their sovereignty and their right to collect taxes. In return, they would be granted a 'privy purse' which was essentially an annuity from the government. Rather grudgingly, all princely states large and small agreed to join the Union of India, except Hyderabad. In June 1947, the Nizam issued a *Firman* or a proclamation declaring independence from the Indian Union.

On the 15th of August 1947, India attained independence from the British, but Hyderabad stood defiant as an independent state. On 29th November 1947, the Nizam signed a 'standstill agreement' with the Indian Union for a period of one year on the advice of Lord Mountbatten. In November 1947, the Government of India appointed K M Munshi, the Agent General of India in Hyderabad.

In the months following the signing of the Standstill Agreement, suspicion and misgivings between the Nizam and the Indian government grew. Relations between the two were far from amicable. The Razakar Movement, supported by the *Majlis Ittehad-ul-Musalmeen*, supporting Islamic supremacy in southern India gained ground in Hyderabad. Led by the zealous Kasim Razvi, the *Razakars* compelled the Nizam to maintain his independence and not relent to pressure from the Indian government. Claiming his right to remain independent in accordance with the Indian Independence Act, the Nizam declared Hyderabad a free, self-governing, independent state but the Government of India refused to accept his point of view.

Sardar Vallabhbhai Patel, the deputy Prime Minister of India termed Hyderabad as 'cancer

The Hyderabad flag is lowered and the Indian tricolour is hoisted at the Bolarum Residency, Secunderabad, 1948

in the belly of India'. On the 21st of June 1948, Lord Mountbatten left India without resolving the Hyderabad issue. Sardar Patel insisted that the state had to merge with the Indian union and to further tighten the noose, an economic blockade was imposed.

Mir Osman Ali Khan with the Union Home Minister Sardar Vallabh bhai Patel and Major General JN Chowdhary, the Military Governor, 1949

On the 10th of September 1948, the Nizam sent Nawab Moin Nawaz Jung to the Security Council to represent Hyderabad's case before the United Nations. This was the last straw. All channels of communication were severed and the Government of India contemplated military action against the defiant state.

The Police Action

Ye jung hai jung-i-azadi,
Azadi ke parcham tale......

This war is a war of independence,
Under the shadow of freedom .....

Maqdoom Mohiuddin, Hyderabad's celebrated inspirational poet gave this soul stirring clarion call 57 years ago. Many young men were inspired to join the struggle to liberate Hyderabad.

On the 13th of September 1948, the Indian Army initiated its Police Action against Hyderabad. The exercise was termed Operation

Polo and for five days the *Razakars* and the Hyderabad army made a half hearted attempt to resist the Indian army. But their antiquated ammunition and ill equipped soldiers were no match to an entire armoured division of the mighty Indian army commanded by Lieutenant General Maharaj Shri Rajendra Singhji, GOC-in-C Southern Command and Major General JN Chowdhary GOC of the Armoured Division. A number of Razakars lost their lives in the battle and their feeble resistance was soon overcome. Five days later, on the 18th of September, 1948, the Indian army entered Secunderabad Cantonment. Military rule was imposed and Major General JN Chowdhary was appointed the Military Governor of Hyderabad. A reluctant Hyderabad finally merged with the Indian Union. For a smooth transition and to placate the sentiments of the hurt *Hyderabadis*, the Government of India considered it prudent to appoint Osman Ali Khan as the *Rajpramukh* of Hyderabad state, a position that he held from 26th January 1950 to 31st October 1956.

Democracy had the whole world in its grip and how long could Hyderabad stay unaffected? The boundary of this region in the Deccan was redrawn on linguistic considerations. The Marathi speaking areas merged with

Qasim Rizvi with the Razakars at a parade in Malakpet, 1948

Mir Osman Ali Khan with Dr Burgula Ramakrishna,1955

Maharashtra, the Kannada speaking region with Karnataka and on 1st November 1956, the Telugu speaking areas along with the region formerly known as Andhra formed the new state of Andhra Pradesh with Hyderabad as its capital.

Mir Osman Ali Khan withdrew completely from public life and chose to lead a quiet, secluded life with his family. He had wisely formed a number of trusts that took care of his family's needs and funded his various charitable institutions.

Osman Ali Khan greets Dr C Rajgopalachari, the Governor General of India, 1949

In 1967 Osman Ali Khan passed away and his eldest grandson, Mukarram Jah, became the new Nizam – a designation that had no meaning, no duties and no responsibilities any more. In 1972, the Indian Prime Minister, Ms Indira Gandhi abolished the 'privy purse' and monarchs and royal families lost all their privileges at one go. Mukarram Jah migrated to Australia and later Turkey, and while most of his estate is being managed by the trusts formed by his grandfather, some of it has been acquired by the government.

Thus an era became history and a dynasty spanning seven generations faded into the twilight leaving behind an indelible print on the sand of time.

Mir Osman Ali Khan – an enigma

'Zikr kya, hosh, ankhon pe kisike Osman,
Jigar-o-dil bhi qurban kiye baithein hain'

'What do I say about Osman Ali Khan? I could give my heart and life for him', wrote Syed Ali Hasan, in praise of Osman Ali Khan, the last Nizam of Hyderabad. Acclaimed as the richest man of his time, Osman Ali Khan was truly an enigma. He acquired phenomenal wealth and his fortune amounted to at least £100 million in gold and silver bullion and £400 million in jewels. His bedroom was stacked with chests heaped with coins and precious jewellery. The ruler of the biggest princely state in India, he was the only one to merit the title 'His Exalted Highness' from the British crown.

In the first half of the 20th century, he ruled a state the size of Italy with absolute authority.

A frail man with a firm mind, the seventh Nizam was a skilled administrator. He coined his own money, printed his own stamps and provided a major railway network, public transport and airways to the people of Hyderabad. He even had his own private army called the Hyderabad Regular Forces comprising of twenty five thousand men commanded by local and British officers. Due to his kindness and tolerance, a large population of Hindus moved into Hyderabad from the neighbouring states.

Osman Ali Khan was a philanthropist and donated generously. If he donated a large sum to the Aligarh Muslim University, he also contributed generously to the Hindu University at Benaras. In 1924, he gladly met the entire expense of the electrification of the holy city of Mecca.

However, unlike his extravagant father, he denied himself the pleasures of a good life. He

Osman Ali Khan with his family

Prince Mukarram, Asif Jah VIII at his coronation in 1946

was a frugal eater and smoked the cheapest cigarettes. While the best of cars and carriages languished in the garage, he rode an old battered Humber. He wore a scruffy old *fez* (cap) for thirty years, while his worn out slippers were bought for a few rupees locally. He used the same walking stick for close to forty years. In 1946, the Diwan of Hyderabad brought a distinguished

The throne today displayed at Purani Haveli

Persian visitor to the Nizam's court. He introduced the visitor to the Nizam, and said reverently in Persian, '*Een Shah-i-Dekhan ast!*' (This is the King of the Deccan). The startled visitor exclaimed, '*Panah-ba-khuda!*' (God save us!) While philanthropy was his religion and prudence his conviction, extravagance was a word deliberately excluded from Osman Ali Khan's lexicon!

A royal announcement made in the 1950's declared that anyone who had worked for the Nizam or was associated with the royal family would be adopted by the Nizam's Trust and benefit from it. They were the *Khanazads* or the permanent beneficiary of the Nizam's estates. One such *Khanazad* is an old woman now in her eighties who had worked in the royal palace. Today, her son earns well and she doesn't need the money from the Nizam's trust. Yet for the past fifteen years, every week, the old woman carries flowers to the tomb of her beloved Nizam. This simple gesture shows how much the *Hyderabadis* loved their last Nizam!

The central hall of the Chowmahalla Palace

ARCHITECTURE OF THE ASIF JAHS

The Chowmahalla Palace

The Chowmahalla palace or the four palaces, was built by Salabat Jung, the third son of Asif Jah 1. The oldest of the Asifjahi palaces, the Chowmahalla is sprawled over sixty acres of land. The palaces were built around an enchanting garden with a fountain in the middle. The Durbar Hall on the north was where dignitaries like the British Viceroys were entertained while the palace on the southern side was used for receiving nobles and the state officials. The western palace was the Nizam's personal living quarter and the eastern palace housed the offices of the Nizam.

Fashioned after the Shah of Persia's palace in Tehran, the Chowmahalla underwent renovations and expansion ever so often, acquiring a variegated architecture. The Panch Mahal, Rang Mahal, Afzal Mahal, Aftab Mahal and several other *havelis* were added over the years. The entire complex later got the name Khilwat Mahal.

The interior of the palace was a blend of different periods and styles. The rooms were done in different colours with matching grand Turkish and Venetian chandeliers. The halls were decorated with beautiful French furnishings, rich tapestry and elaborate drapes. The banquets held in Chowmahalla were so lavish that it took the servants a month to just clean the crockery and the garden was so beautiful that the Prince of Wales who visited the palace in 1922, wrote that it could easily compare with 'one of the enchanted gardens of the Arabian Nights.'

The fifth, sixth and the seventh Nizams were coronated here. Over the years, this majestic palace of the Nizams lost its grandeur. Due to the efforts of Princess Esra, wife of Prince Mukarram Jah, work was initiated to restore the palace's lost splendour. In January 2005, after a long long time the garden bloomed once again, fountains came alive and the doors of the refurbished palace were opened to visitors.

The Falaknuma Palace

Sir Vicar-ul-Umara was a great patron of art, architecture and education. During his tenure as the Prime Minister, he started the education department, an engineering school, a law school, the Legislative Council, the Asifia State Library now known as the State Central Library and introduced numerous administrative reforms. Sir Viqar also built the Begumpet railway station near his palace to avoid travelling into the city whenever he needed to make a train journey.

Sir Vicarul Umara was a passionate builder and it was his fascination with Palladian villas and the stately English homes that led to the creation of Falaknuma, or 'the mirror of the sky'. Better than all other palaces of its time, the Falaknuma could easily compare with the palace at Versailles.

Work began on this magnificent structure in 1884 and was completed nine years later. Sir Vicar had followed his dream, but the palace of his dreams left him completely bankrupt. Built at a cost of over four million, the Falaknuma was the last word in grandeur and opulence. With an estate of over three hundred acres, the palace stood on a hill two hundred feet high, offering a grandstand view of the city from all sides. The building resembled a scorpion with its two stingers. There was the main building in the center while the northern and the southern wings fanned out on both ends. The façade was Grecian, while the front lawn was a replica of an English garden.

The splendid proportions of the building along with the grand white marble staircase, beautifully carved balustrades and the exquisite marble vestibules leave the visitors spellbound. The interior was accessorized with Italian marble, French tapestry, fine Victorian furniture, exquisite crystal chandeliers and paintings. While the marble was imported all the way from Italy, all the chandeliers in the palace were brought from Venice and Belgium. Falaknuma boasted of the largest chandelier in the city.

The majestic Banquet Hall, with an enormous rosewood table that could seat a hundred and two guests at a time, is stunning. Artists from Florence worked on the ceiling and lined it with leather while nuns from France used camel hide to upholster the furniture in the hall. The Nizam sat in the middle, on a chair whose armrest was

The dining table that could seat a hundred and two guests at a time

The palace interiors

The grand marble staircase leads to the upper chambers

two inches higher than the others. While the organ played in the background, the honoured guests were served dinner in gold plates and fine crystal gold rimmed goblets held wine. Four hundred servants waited in attendance.

A number of other rooms like the card room, the Billiard room, the smoking suites, etc, formed the side wings of the building. A curio cabinet in the formal living room displayed priceless jewels and artifacts including a three feet high silver mango tree, Dresden china and a fabulous jade collection. The library was styled after the library at Windsor Castle with an intricately carved walnut ceiling. An incredible collection of books and manuscripts all bound in Moroccon leather, lined the shelves of the library. The library displayed an astounding collection of the Holy Quran collected from all over the world. Also exhibited was a priceless piece - the eighteen pages of the Quran stained with the blood of Caliph Osman II who was killed while writing it.

The palace boasted of electrical switchboards, telephones and every modern fixture one could think of. When Queen Mary visited the palace in 1906, she was surprised to see that the jets in the bathroom sprayed perfume. The bathrooms had showers, bathtubs styled like a modern day jacuzzi and imported toilet paper. The wash basins were made of crystal while jugs in sterling silver adorned the restroom.

Some of the distinguished guests who stayed in this splendid palace were King GeorgeV of England, Queen Mary, Prince and Princess of Wales, the Dukes of Austria and Russia along with several British Viceroys, Governor Generals and nobles. When Sir Winston Churchill who served in the Secunderabad cantonment expressed his desire to see the palace, Sir Vicar invited his entire regiment for a banquet at the palace.

In 1895 Nizam Mahboob Ali Pasha, the sixth Nizam, visited the palace for a day but stayed on for twenty days. He was floored by the grace and grandeur of Falaknuma and expressed his admiration to Sir Vicar. Sir Vicar had barely stayed in his dream house for five years but had no choice but to gift it to the Nizam. The Nizam more than compensated for the cost of the building. Mahboob Ali Pasha moved in with his family while the Prime Minister moved out into one of his palaces in the city.

The Nizam lived there till 1911. It was at Falaknuma that Mahboob Ali Pasha breathed his last.

The King Kothi

The seventh Nizam, Mir Osman Ali Khan, lived in King Kothi, a palace bought by his father Mahboob Ali Pasha who had a penchant for buying ostentatious homes. This grand palace was owned by a noble, Kamal Khan who in a display of flamboyance had his initials KK imprinted on all the furniture, crockery, windows and even the iron grilles of the palace. Mahboob Ali Pasha was keen to possess the palace but the bold engraving of the owner's initials made him a little wary. A courtier, to his relief, came up with an intelligent solution. He suggested that a house in Urdu was called a *Kothi* and since it would thereafter be the king's palace it could be renamed King Kothi or the King's Palace justifying the engraved initials. The Nizam was pleased and went ahead and bought the palace. He compensated the owner with a *Jagir* that covered the cost of the palace many times over.

The King Kothi campus has several palaces within it including Nazri Bagh, the palace where the seventh Nizam lived.

In the background is a picture of a jadli taken at Paigah Tombs

The Paigah Tombs

The affluence of the wealthy Paigah nobles is mirrored in their tombs at Santoshnagar, on the city outskirts. In both grandeur and style, the Paigah tombs easily match the tombs of the Egyptians and the tombs of the rulers of the Ming dynasty. In sharp contrast to the rather austere tombs of the Nizams of Hyderabad, these were elaborately designed and intricately embellished.

The main structure is a rectangular single storeyed arcade. This area houses the tomb of the most illustrious of the Paigah nobles. On top of the structure, modelled in stucco are thin stem-like columns ending in pineapple shaped domes. Rosettes, floral motifs, Chinese patterns and arabesques in stucco adorn the tombs. The stucco is either in relief or intaglio and measure upto three centimeters in thickness. Very similar to the interiors of the eighteenth century French palaces and hotels, the fine detailing and workmanship of the tombs is amazing. Some of the tombs inside the arcade are in marble and studded with semi-precious stones. The exquisite craftsmanship of the screens or the *Jaalis* in an array of geometrical patterns is noteworthy.

There is another smaller rectangular area which holds the tombs of the lesser known nobles. Within three hundred meters of this, lies the burial area where the womenfolk and the mistresses of the Paigah nobles rest. One tomb that deserves mention is the tomb of Sir Asman Jah. The beautiful tomb is open to the sky as his name '*Asman*' in Urdu means sky.

The Paigah tombs include distinct Hindu elements such as the Rajput style *Jharokhas*. European elements were incorporated by nobles like Sir Asman Jah and Sir Viqar-ul-Umara who had travelled extensively and were fascinated by the grace of Italian architecture.

These tombs are a repository of great architectural style and give an enchanting glimpse of the life and times of the Paigah nobles.

Purani Haveli

The Purani Haveli, or the old mansion as it literally means, was a part of the estate of Mir Momin, the Prime Minister of Muhammad Quli Qutub Shah. In 1777, the second Nizam, Mir Nizam Ali Khan acquired some of the estate from Rukn-ud-Daula, a descendant of Mir Momin. The palace that stands today was built for the third Nizam, Sikander Jah. Sikander Jah later moved from here and the palace was in disuse for a long time. It now began to be called Haveli Khadeem. The fifth Nizam was born in Purani Haveli and lived here. During his time the haveli regained some of its lost splendour. The sixth Nizam, Mahboob Ali Pasha too, was born here and spent his childhood at the Purani Haveli. He contributed a great deal to restore the old glory of the haveli. Mahboob Ali Pasha and later his son, Osman Ali Khan, added several wings to the old palace. Though, Osman Ali Khan later moved to King Kothi, he visited Purani Haveli almost every day, to meet his ailing mother.

An interesting event associated with the palace was the firing of guns three times a day to indicate time, a practice that continued till the 1950's. Another remarkable feature of the palace is the 240 ft long wooden wardrobe, the largest running wardrobe in the world, built to accommodate Mahboob Ali Pasha's extensive collection of clothes, shoes and accessories. A part of the Purani Haveli has been now converted into a museum. The exotic locale of the palace formed a perfect backdrop for the Merchant Ivory film, Heat and Dust.

The British Residency: A new landmark

In 1800, James Achilles Kirkpatrick obtained permission for the construction of a suitable home for the British Resident. The Nizam was shocked when he was shown an elaborate plan of the proposed building, drawn on a large sheet. He assumed that the Resident planned a house larger than his, hence refused to grant permission for construction. The wise Prime Minister understood that the Nizam was unaware of the intricacies of architectural drawings and quietly advised Kirkpatrick to get a smaller plan made. In the next Durbar, the smart Resident presented the Nizam with the plan drawn on a postcard. The relieved Nizam immediately agreed to bear the entire expense of the construction of the British Residency.

Sixty three acres of land along the Musi River was allotted for the Residency. The design and the construction were supervised by Lieutenant S Russel of the Madras Engineers. Work on the project began in 1803 and ended in 1809. The charm of the building lies in its neo-classical style, specially the stairs that seems to be an imitation of the staircase of the Home House at Portman Square, London, built by Robert Adam in 1777. An elegant, lion-flanked flight of twenty steps leads to the main building. The northern façade has a majestic porch supported by imposing Corinthian columns. The interiors designed in a Grecian style have rich Roman ornamentation and in front was a beautiful lawn, fashioned after an English garden. The building has grand proportions with luxurious rooms, imposing halls and galleries where the Resident used to entertain in style. For the first time, a *Zenana* was built for the Muslim bride of the British Resident. Today the Residency houses the Koti Women's College and is a treasured heritage monument.

High Court

The High Court

On the southern bank of the Musi river stands the High Court of Andhra Pradesh, a stately structure built in the Saracenic style by the seventh Nizam, Mir Osman Ali Khan. The plan was made by an architect from Jaipur and executed by a local engineer, Mehar Ali Fazil. Work on the splendid structure started in April 1915 and was completed by March 1919. The silhouette of the domes against the evening sun presents a spectacular picture.

The Jubilee Hall

Amidst the verdant lawns of the Public Gardens stands the Jubilee Hall. It was built as a part of the Silver Jubilee Celebration held to celebrate the completion of twenty five years of Osman Ali Khan's reign. Earlier a simple Durbar Hall stood here, but in 1937, the old structure was pulled down and the imposing Jubilee Hall built in its place. Built essentially in the Indo-Persian style, the main hall has been richly embellished. Grand chandeliers light up the hall imparting a splendid glow to the interior.

Today, the Jubille Hall is used for state banquets and also serves as a venue for important conferences.

An aerial view of Osmania General Hospital

The Osmania General Hospital

At the behest of the City Improvement Board of Mir Osman Ali Khan, Osmania General Hospital was built on the bank of Musi. The year was 1925 and the hospital sprawled over a twenty seven acre estate. Initially the strength was four hundred and fifty, but today it is a thousand bed hospital and one of the largest in Andhra Pradesh. The imposing structure with its splendid high domes beautifully compliments the High Court building near by.

The Salar Jung Museum

On display at the Salar Jung Museum in Hyderabad, is one of the world's largest private art collections of one discerning art lover, Nawab Salar Jung III, the Prime Minister of Hyderabad. A distinguished noble, Salar Jung III was a judicious collector and during his lifetime assimilated a treasure trove of priceless art, unmatched in quality and diversity.

The veiled Rebecca

Around forty three thousand pieces of art, fifty thousand books, nine thousand manuscripts, eighty original European paintings, a handwritten miniature Quran, carpets woven with metallic ivory thread, Noor Jehan's dagger, Jehangir's wine glass, Aurungzeb's sword - the collection is astounding! Rare manuscripts, curios in jade, Japanese silk paintings and around three hundred walking sticks are also a part of this amazing collection. A collection of three hundred clocks and watches too find a place here, of which the most popular is the musical clock from an English company, Cook and Kelvy. A mechanical marvel, the clock is the star attraction at the museum where hundreds throng every day to watch a toy soldier emerge from a door to strike the gong every hour.

As passion for collection ran in the family, the museum displays the collection not only of Salar Jung III, but also those of his ancestors Salar Jung I and II. The veiled Rebecca, an exquisite translucent marble statue of a woman by Bezoni, an Italian sculptor, and a nineteenth century wooden statue of Margaretta and Mephistopheles by an unknown artist, are the star attraction at the museum and belong to Salar Jung I. Initially the museum was housed in the hundred year old family palace called the Diwan Devdi, but in 1968 it was moved to the present building on the bank of Musi River. Nearly ten lakh visitors visit the museum annually. In 1961, by an Act of Parliament, the museum was declared 'an institution of national importance'.

Secunderabad Club

The historic Secunderabad Club

The Secunderabad Club was the last outpost of the British Raj built initially as a residence for the Prime Minister, Salar Jung I. In 1878, Salar Jung donated it to the local representatives of the British Civil Service who converted it into an elitist club for their officers. More than a hundred and twenty five years later, it still retains its exclusivity and is the most reputed club in the city.

The Tomb of Raymond

General Raymond, a Republican French mercenary had loyally served the Nizam. His tomb is situated near Asmangadh where back then, the French garrison was stationed. The tomb has a hundred and eighty feet tall granite obelisk and to its left is a shrine styled after a Grecian temple with a pavilion supported by twenty eight pillars. The monument has been recently refurbished to honour the valiant French soldier who was a true *Hyderabadi* at heart.

The Jagirdar College or the present day Hyderabad Public School

The Jagirdar College was established in November 1923 at the initiative of Mr H Wakefield, the chief of the Court of Wards under the Nizam, for the education of the sons of *Jagirdars* and other nobility. After the abolition of the Jagirdari System in 1950, the Government of India converted it into an independent public school. Built in an Indo Islamic style, the stately structure stands on a hundred and forty acre campus. Today many new wings have been added to the original building.

The Legislative Assembly of Andhra Pradesh

Work on this impressive monument began in 1905 to commemorate the fortieth birthday of the sixth Nizam, Mahboob Ali Pasha. The people of Hyderabad had raised money to build this structure. Completed in 1913, it was used as the Town Hall of the old Hyderabad state. Architects from Rajasthan were commissioned for this job which is a happy blend of Rajasthani and Persian architecture. Today this imposing monument houses the Andhra Pradesh Legislative Assembly. New wings have been added to meet the ever growing demand of the Assembly.

The Malakpet Race Course

The Malakpet Racecourse was built more than a century ago and the first race was held here in the winter of 1879. The Grand Pavilion was built in the same year for Mahboob Ali Pasha and members of the royal family. The Nizam came to the racecourse on days when the horses from the royal stables competed. Betting was an amusement for the commoners' and was not permitted in the Grand Pavilion.

Today, this racecourse is one of the most modern in the country and boasts of a swimming pool for the horses and a training school for the jockeys.

The exasperating traffic and the ugly buildings and hoardings that now clutter Abids, have ruined the spirit of the fashion street of old Hyderabad.

The Holy Trinity Church at Bolaram

In 1846, the church of the Holy Trinity at Bolaram was built by General Fraser, the British Resident at Hyderabad. Land for the church was donated by the Nizam while the fund for construction came from Queen Victoria. In November 1983, on a trip to Hyderabad, Queen Elizabeth II along with Prince Philip, visited this church.

The Osman Sagar and the Himayat Sagar Lake

The Osman Sagar and the Himayat Sagar were the two water bodies built during the time of Mir Osman Ali Khan, the seventh Nizam, to augment the water supply in the city. Planned after the floods of 1908, these two lakes were created to check the flooding of the Musi River. Till today, these two reservoirs are the major source of drinking water for the city.

Mir Alam Tank

The Mir Alam Tank was built in 1806 by Mir Alam, the great grand father of Salar Jung 1, the Prime Minister of Hyderabad. It was to serve as a source of drinking water for the city of Hyderabad. The reward money that Mir Alalm received from the Nizam after defeating Tipu Sultan in the Fourth Mysore War, went into the construction of this tank. It was built under the supervision of Sir Henry Russell of Royal Engineers. The mile long bund along the tank with twenty one granite arches was called 'the Queen's necklace.' 'In the name of God it flows and thank God it glides along (1221 A.H)', reads a Persian inscription on the side of the tank.

The Abids Circle in 1924

The store that Abid built at Mustafa Road

MACCA MASJID
PAID PARKING

THE NOBILITY

Hyderabad in the nineteenth and twentieth century was the largest princely state in the country with a very feudal socio-economic framework, as most of the land in the state was held by the landlords called *Jagirdars* and the *Rajas* of the *Samasthans*. The Paigahs, the Salar Jungs the Hindu Rajas and other important nobles constituted the very large aristocracy.

The Paigahs

Sir Viqar-ul-Umara

The Paigahs were the highest in the heirarchy and the most important nobles of Hyderabad. *Pai* means foot and *Gah* place and the term literally meant that the place of these nobles was at the ruler's feet. Gradually, the Paigahs grew to be the most revered and influential of all nobles. Official documents say that Paigahas were the Nizam's household troops or the guards recruited to strengthen the military.

The Paigah nobles trace their origin to Fareed Shakur, a renowned mystic who was buried in Pakpattan in the Punjab region of Pakistan. Like Chengiz Khan, the Seljuks, the Ottomans and the Mughals, the Paigahs were essentially nomads. Descendants of Abul Khair Khan, a noble from the north who came and settled in the Deccan, they moved to Hyderabad in the mid-eighteenth century. Around this time, Abul Khair Khan's son, Abul Fateh Khan, was appointed the Commander-in-Chief of around twelve thousand troops including cavalry and infantry and was granted *Jagirs* in Berar, Hyderabad and Bijapur. He was also conferred the title of Shams-ul-Umara which later became the family name of the Paigahs. He was entrusted the responsibility of defending the state which became a tradition of the Paigah nobles. He raised three million per annum as revenue for the maintenance of the troops.

Linked by marital ties to the Nizams as most Paigah men married the daughters of the Nizams, the Paigah nobles were raised to the exalted status of the blue blooded patricians. Such was their influence that the head of the Paigah family ranked next only to the Nizam.

They were permitted to use their own revenue stamps, appoint their own revenue officials and establish educational institutions. The annual income of the Paigah family in the later years was nearly 5.2 million!

Sir Khurshid Jah Bahadur, a Paigah noble

Nawab Sir Asman Jah Bahadur

The Paigahs promoted art, literature and sports. The *Deori* (mansion) of Sir Asman Jah, the Khurshid Jah palace, Viqar-ul-Umara palace and the Basheer Bagh palace were a few of the important buildings of the time. The one and only Falaknuma was built by Sir Viqar ul Umara . The Paigahs loved sports and the prestigious Nawab Moin-ud-Daula Cup Cricket Tournament was started by Nawab Moin-ud-Daula Bahadur, a keen sportsman and an ardent cricket fan.

The Salar Jungs

The Salar Jungs were the leading Shia nobles of Hyderabad next in hierarchy to the Paigahs. They were the descendants of Shaikh Owais-i-Qarani of Madina, Arabia. In the seventeenth century, this family migrated to Bijapur in India and served first the Mughals and later the Nizams of Hyderabad.

Nawab Dargah Quli Khan, Salar Jung Bahadur, was fourteen years old when Nizam-ul-Mulk granted him a *Jagir*. His influence grew during the reign of the later Nizams. The Salar Jungs were the descendants of Ali Zaman Khan Ghayur Jung, grandson of Dargah Quli Khan. Ghayur Jung succeeded his father-in-law, Mir Alam, as the Prime Minister of Hyderabad. The family enjoyed tremendous power as five members from the family served as Prime Ministers of Hyderabad.

Sir Salar Jung I

Mir Turab Ali Khan Salar Jung I

Mir Turab Ali Khan, Salar Jung I, was an administrator par excellence and shaped the destiny of modern day Hyderabad. He served as the Prime Minister of Hyderabad for thirty years and met the administrative challenges of the state with great resolve.

Salar Jung I was an advocate of modern education and at his behest, a number of institutions like the Dar-ul-Uloom, an Oriental College and a Medical School were started in the state. He was instrumental in the abolition of capital punishment, the practice of *Sati* and the separation of the civil from criminal judiciary. He helped establish a number of courts in the city and the districts.

Salar Jung I had great political acumen and very early in his career, he realized the advantage of supporting the British. Due to unflinching British support, he survived many court intrigues and in 1869, when the three years old Mahboob Ali Khan was coronated as the Nizam, Salar Jung I along with Shams-ul-Umara was appointed Regent and effectively administered the state on behalf of the minor Nizam.

Salar Jung I streamlined the state's finances by establishing a Central Treasury and a Board of Revenue. He started the system of *Zillabandi* to collect revenue from the districts. In 1857, he abolished all privately owned mints and introduced a new currency for Hyderabad called the '*Hali Sicca*'. With his initiative, various government departments like Forest, Revenue, Customs, Postal and Mint were totally revamped. In 1860, the districts of Raichur and Naldurg were restored to the Nizam yielding 2.1 million as revenue to the government. In 1863, a severe famine stared Hyderabad in its face and poverty and hunger killed hundreds. To tide over the crisis, Salar Jung took a loan of two crore from the British and carried on relief operation till the situation eased.

Salar Jung I should be credited for linking Hyderabad by railway with the three presidency towns of India and extending the railways to the remotest corners of the state.

When Salar Jung I passed away on 7th February 1883, the state mourned the loss of a brilliant administrator and a great statesman.

Mir Laiq Ali Khan Salar Jung II

Mir Laiq Ali Khan succeeded his father and was appointed the new Prime Minister by the sixth Nizam, Mir Mahboob Ali Khan. After three years in power, he became the victim of a vicious campaign started by the other nobles that eventually cost him his job. The Nizam forced him to step down and the disappointed noble went on a long tour of Europe. He died an unhappy man in 1889.

Mir Yousuf Ali Khan Salar Jung III

Mir Yousuf Ali Khan was the only child of Laiq Ali Khan and lost his father just a month after his birth. The sixth Nizam, Mir Mahboob Ali Khan, took the responsibility of bringing up the young child and groomed him to be the Prime Minister of Hyderabad. He was conferred the title of Salar Jung at an elaborate ceremony at the Chowmahalla Palace by Mahboob Ali Khan. Mir Osman Ali Khan, the seventh Nizam, entrusted Salar Jung with complete administrative control over his state. In July 1912, when Maharaj Sir Kishen Pershad resigned, the Nizam appointed Yousuf Ali Khan the new Prime Minister of Hyderabad.

Salar Jung III however, was not destined to be as popular as his grandfather. Citing personal reasons, Salar Jung III chose to resign from his post in 1914. He was a great connoisseur of art and started collecting art when he was barely nine years old. After relinquishing the post of the Prime Minister, he devoted all his time and energy towards collecting the rarest of art, antiques and manuscripts from the world over. Salar Jung III's twelve palaces and estates spread all over the country, were filled with priceless art and only a part of the entire collection is exhibited at the Salarjung Museum in Hyderabad.

His collection, along with the priceless collectibles of his father and grandfather, is an eternal legacy to his beloved city.

The Hindu Rajas of the Samasthans

The *Rajas* of the Hindu *Samasthans* (estates) were another major segment of the nobility that thrived during the Nizams. These Rajas were essentially *Zamindars* (landlords) and military chieftains who had successfully established their authority over the surrounding areas. They were also known as *Paligars* and their territory, *Palayam*. These *Rajas* trace their origin to the ancient Hindu kingdom of Warangal and survived for nearly six centuries.

During the time of the Asif Jahs, these Rajas paid a sum to the Nizam according to the size of their land holding. In times of war they were expected to provide military assistance to the Nizam. While the smaller land holdings withered away, especially after the massive exercise of administrative reforms undertaken by Salar Jung I, the bigger *Zamindars* (landlords) carried on as *Rajas* of the *Samasthans*. These *Rajas* were treated with respect in the Nizam's court and some of them even enjoyed the liberty to mint their own coins and print stamps. They exercised both civil and criminal jurisdiction over their territory. There were about sixteen *Samasthans* that survived till the time of Independence and the most notable of them were Gadwal, Wanaparthi, Jatprol, Amarchinta, Palvancha, Gurgunta, Gopalpet and Anagundi.

The Gadwal Samasthan

Raja of Gadwal

Situated between the Tungabhadra and Krishna rivers and spread over an area of eight hundred square miles, the Gadwal *Samasthan* was one of the most important *Samasthan*. The rulers of Gadwal had supported the Mughal emperor, Aurungzeb, in his battle against Bijapur and Golconda. In 1724, the Raja shifted his loyalty to the Nizam of Hyderabad and gained cognizance as his trusted ally. Raja Ram Bhupal, the Raja of Gadwal, was honoured in the court of the second Nizam. He was granted the privilege to mint his own currency and the '*Peshkash*' or offering that he made to the Nizam, was in Gadwal rupees.

Wanaparthy Samsthan

Logo of Raja Rameshwar Rao of Wanapurthy Samasthan

Wanaparthy was another important *Samasthan* spread over six hundred and forty square miles in the district of Mahboobnagar. This *Samasthan* had been in existence since the time of the Vijaynagar Empire. The early Rajas maintained an army of two thousand infantry and two

Raja of Wanaparthy

thousand cavalry. They too enjoyed the privilege to mint their own coins. Nizam-ul-Mulk, Asif Jah I, was very close to Gopal Rao, the Raja of Wanaparthy. The Wanaparthy Raja rendered valuable service during the Sepoy Mutiny – a part of India's freedom struggle, supporting the Nizam and the British. The sixth Nizam, Mahboob Ali Pasha acknowledged the constant support of Raja Rameshwar Rao and honoured him with the title of *Maha Bhupal*. The seventh Nizam, Osman Ali Khan conferred the title of *Maharaja* on him. They continued to be a loyal and able ally of the Nizam till Independence.

The Samasthan of Jatprol

This was the oldest *Samasthan* and had great historical significance. Pillalamarri Bethala Reddy was not only the founder of this Samasthan but had also helped establish the families of *Rajas* of Bobbilli, Pitthapore (Pithapuram) in Godavari district, Malleshwaram in Krishna district and Venkatgiri in Nellore district. Bethala Reddy was a feudal lord owing allegiance to the *Raja* of Warangal. It was only in 1507 that this *Samasthan* received recognition from the *Raja* of Vijaynagar.

Nizam Ali Khan, Asif Jah II, acknowledged the then Raja of Jatprol, Bari Gudupala Rao and awarded him a *mansab* and a title of Raja Bahadur. Raja Venkat Laxman Rao Bahadur was a remarkable ruler who brought about significant social and civic reforms in the administration.

The Hindu nobility

The Nizams nobility comprised of some Hindu nobles on whom he conferred the titles of *Raja* and *Maharaja*. The entire Hindu nobility rose from the rank of *Peshkars* or revenue officials and a few rose to the rank of the Prime Minister of Hyderabad. Most of these nobles belonged to the family of Rai Mulchand, Raja Ram Baksh and Raja Narender Pershad.

Hindu nobles during the Asif Jahi time

Maharaja Chandulal

Maharaja Chandulal Bahadur

Rai Mulchand, a descendant of Raja Todar Mal of the Mughal Emperor Akbar's court, had accompanied Nizam-ul-Mulk to the Deccan. Nizam-ul-Mulk was impressed with his capability and appointed him the head of Customs and Excise. Chandulal was the great grand son of Rai Mulchand. He started his career as a supervisor of Nawab Shamsher Jung's *jagir* and due to his competence and perseverance rose to the rank of *Peshkar* and later the Prime Minister of the state. After holding several important posts, Maharaja Chandulal resigned in September 1843.

Raja Ram Baksh

In 1843, Raja Ram Baksh was appointed *Peshkar* by the Nizam. He was the nephew of Raja Chandulal and son of Raja Govind Baksh. After three years into the job, citing personal reasons Ram Baksh resigned. Again after three years, the fourth Nizam summoned him and appointed him *Peshkar*. He was also entrusted with the job of a *Vakil* or intermediary between the Nizam and the British Resident. In November 1849 he was promoted as the Prime Minister of the state but retired a year later in 1850.

Maharaja Narain Pershad Narender Bahadur

Maharaja Narender Pershad was the grandson of Chandu Lal. In 1853, when Sir Salar Jung became the Prime Minister of Hyderabad, Narender Pershad was appointed *Peshkar*. He helped avert an attack on the British Residency by insurgents. In the absence of Salar Jung I, he officiated as the Prime Minister and after Sir Salar Jung's death, he was given the exalted status of the senior-most administrator of the state.

The sixth Nizam trusted Raja Narender Pershad and requested him to receive the Governor General when he visited Raichur. The Nizam conferred him with the title of *Maharaja* and also included him as a member of the newly constituted Council of State.

Maharaja Kishen Pershad Bahadur

Raja Narender Pershad did not have a son and the heir apparent was his grandson, Kishen Pershad Bahadur. Proficient in both Arabic and Persian, he was barely ten years old when he was conferred the title of *Raja Bahadur*.

In 1892 Kishen Pershad was appointed *Peshkar* by the sixth Nizam and was also given command of the army. In the year 1901, he officiated as the Prime Minister of the state in the absence of Sir Viqar-ul-Umara. The very next year, he was formally appointed the Prime Minister of Hyderabad . His competence, tact and authority was unmatched. His proximity to the Nizam gave him complete control over the administration. When Lord Curzon came to Hyderabad, he visited Raja Kishen Pershad to view a parade from his home. The Raja also played host to the Prince and Princess of Wales at his palace. Appreciating his loyalty, the British government awarded the title of 'Knight Commander of the order of the Indian Empire' on the *Raja*.

During his term of ten years, Maharaja Kishen Pershad strengthened the administration and restructured the state's finance. In July 1912, during the reign of the seventh Nizam, Kishen Pershad resigned from the post of the Prime Minister but continued as the *Peshkar* of the state.

A great scholar of Persian and Arabic, the *Maharaja* authored several books and was also an accomplished calligraphist. He was a gifted poet and wrote under the pseudonym *Shad.* Maharaja Kishen Pershad passed away in 1940.

Raja Sham Raj Rajwanth Bahadur

Raja Sham Raj was another prominent noble of Hyderabad state and his family was regarded next in importance only to Raja Kishen Pershad's. Some of his anscestors served as *Peshkars* in the Nizam's court.

Raja Bahadur Bansilal Pittie

Raja Bahadur Bansilal Pittie was an affluent and renowned merchant of Hyderabad. Originally from Jodhpur in Rajputana, the family migrated to Hyderabad and established a flourishing business here. They set up several banks in the city. His wealth and influence won him many friends and the sixth Nizam, Mir Mahboob Ali Khan, conferred the title of Raja Bahadur on him. He was also made a member of the Nizam's Legislative Council and appointed the President of the Trade Union of India. In 1935, *Raja Bahadur* passed away, but the tradition of charity initiated by him was carried forth by his family.

Raja Dhanrajgirji Bahadur

It was in the nineteenth century that Mahadev Gir moved to Hyderabad from Pune in search of better business opportunities. One of the members of his family, Umrao Gir became a successful trader. His wealth made him popular in the social circles of Hyderabad and also in the court. Their trading business flourished and impressed with their accomplishment, the sixth Nizam honoured Raja Gyan Girji Bahadur, a member of the family with the title of *Raja Bahadur*. Raja Dhanraj Gir Bahadur, a scion of the Gir family was renowned for his support to charitable causes. His daughter, Indira Dhanrajgir Sarma is well known in the literary circles of the city.

From the Gir family album, 1904

Raja Deen Dayal

Raja Deen Dayal, an accomplished photographer was engaged by the British Government to document the monuments of Central India. He did it with great skill and his pictures were appreciated by none other than the Queen of England. On a tour of Hyderabad, he met the sixth Nizam, Mahboob Ali Khan. The Nizam was so impressed with his magical skill with the camera, that he appointed him his

Raja DeenDayal

court photographer and lured him to move to Hyderabad. He was granted the title of Musawwir Jung.

In 1885, the firm Raja Deen Dayal and sons was set up in Secunderabad. Deen Dayal captured the many moods of the sixth Nizam apart from documenting important events of his time - political, religious and social. Also chronicled were ceremonies, coronations, royal visits, picnics, parades and Nizam's hunting and pleasure trips. These pictures provide a precious glimpse into the life and times of the Nizam. Portraits were his forte and their quality is truly astounding. In 1892 he started a *Zenana* (women's) studio in Hyderabad in association with an English lady, Ms Levick. The Raja also documented the diplomatic impasse during the Delhi Durbar of 1903 when Mahboob Ali Pasha refused to get down from his royal carriage until an elephant was brought to the platform to take him to the city.

Raja Deen Dayal's legacy was carried on by his sons who kept the family business alive and in the process provided valuable nuggets of pictorial information about the lives and times of the *Hyderabadis* during the Nizams. The pictures of Hyderabad shot by Raja DeenDayal so captivated Jacqueline Kennedy that on her visit to India she couldn't resist but include Hyderabad in her itinerary!

Pic: Raja DeenDayal

Nawab Mir Alam Bahadur

Syed Abdul Qasim Mir Alam Bahadur, a descendant of the distinguished Nuria Saiyeds of Persia, renowned for their contribution to Islamic culture and literature, was one of the most popular Prime Ministers of Hyderabad. His father, Syed Reza, was a great scholar and migrated to Hyderabad during the time of Nizam-ul-Mulk. When the British envoy Johnson visited Hyderabad, Mir Alam served as an intermediary in the negotiations between the second Nizam and the British. When the terms of a peace settlement were being conferred with Tipu Sultan, Nizam Asif Jah II sent Mir Alam to Lord Cornwallis for parleys. In 1804 he was appointed the Prime Minister, a post that he held till his demise in 1808. A great scholar of Persian, he authored '*Insha-i-Alam*'.

Nizam Yar Jung

Mir Asad Ali Khan, Nawab Nizam Yar Jung

One of the eleven *Umra-i-Azam* or the chief nobles, Nawab Nizam Yar Jung was a noble of the highest rank in Hyderabad and enjoyed tremendous respect in the court. His family had migrated from Persia. Sir Salar Jung I took him under his wing and trained him in the art of diplomacy and governance. He was sent to England to pursue his higher education where he had the honour of meeting Queen Victoria. He accompanied the Nizam to the Delhi *Durbar.* He was appointed the Minister of public works and later the military department.

Nawab Fakhr-ul-Mulk

Another luminary and one of the eleven of the elitist Umra-i-Azam was Nawab Fakhr-ul-Mulk Bahadur. His family, like most other members of the nobility, had migrated from Persia. A very close confidante of the Nizam, he accompanied him to the Durbar in Delhi and later Calcutta and Aurangabad. He was a member of the Council of Regency during the time of the sixth Nizam and also worked as Minister for police and the judiciary. He was also a member of the

Cabinet Council and served as the Vice President of the government's Executive Council.

Muhammad Faizuddin Khan Musharraf Jung Bahadur

Muhammad Faizuddin Khan was a native of Hyderabad and a distinguished poet and litterateur. He was granted the title of Musharraf Jung Bahadur by the Nizam for his outstanding contribution in the field of culture and literature, especially towards the growth of Urdu. He authored several books in Urdu and translated some renowned works into Persian.

Nawab Amin Jung Bahadur

Nawab Sir Ahmad Hussain Amin Jung Bahadur

Nawab Sir Ahmad Hussain Amin Jung Bahadur was the first Muslim to obtain a masters degree from Madras University. He served as a Magistrate and Deputy Collector in Madras. Impressed with his academic qualification, the sixth Nizam appointed him his Assistant Secretary. He was later promoted as the Secretary to the Nizam and the Nizam trusted him so much that he would not sign a letter without his advice. Nawab Sir Afsar-ul-Mulk Bahadur and Nawab Sir Amin Jung Bahadur were the most trusted lieutenants of the Nizam's inner coterie and were popularly known as the right and left hand of the sixth Nizam.

Nawab Sir Ahmad Hussain was so loyal to the family that after Mahboob Ali Pasha's death, he was persuaded to continue in his post by the seventh Nizam. After the death of Salar Jung III, he was promoted as the *Peshi* Minister by Nizam Osman Ali Khan, but functioned virtually as the Chief Minister. For six long years he continued as the de facto Chief Minister of the state. His allegiance to the British won him the title of 'Knight Commander of the Most Eminent Order of the Indian Empire'. The seventh Nizam conferred the title of Nawab Amin Jung Bahadur on Sir Ahmad Hussain and included him in the delegation to the Round Table Conference held in London.

Sir Akbar Nazarally Hydari

Sir Akbar Hydari who served in the government of Mahboob Ali Pasha and later Osman Ali Khan, was a skilled administrator. With great efficiency, he organized the state finances, prepared budgets and pooled resources to fund the various welfare programmes of the state.

Sir Hydari was working with the Finance Department of the Government of India when he was invited to Hyderabad by Mahboob Ali Khan. In 1907, he was appointed the finance secretary and later secretary of the judicial, education and the home departments. He was instrumental in coercing the government to complete the construction of the High Court, the City College and also the Osmania Hospital. He raised Rs 1 crore to aid the setting up of new industries in the state and pushed the proposal for Osmania University. He was a great advocate of women's education and it was due to his support that the Mahboobia Girls College came up in the city.

In 1927 the British Monarchy conferred knighthood on Akbar Hydari and in 1931 he represented Hyderabad at the Round Table Conference in London. A great reformer and an adept financial manager, Sir Akbar Nazarally Hydari was one of the greatest administrators of Hyderabad.

Mehdi Nawaz Jung

Syed Muhammad Mehdi was born in 1894 and served as a civil servant in the Nizam's government. In 1926 he was appointed the Cabinet Secretary, a position he held for nearly eleven years. In 1937 he was appointed the Municipal Commissioner of Hyderabad and he undertook the electrification of the entire old city. During his tenure as Commissioner, he initiated the laying of most of the city roads along with creating a drainage system for

the city. Due to his initiative, the Niloufer Children's Hospital and the Cancer Hospital were built. After entering electoral politics, he served in the cabinet of N Sanjiva Reddy and was later appointed the Governor of Gujarat.

A very warm and sociable man, Mehdi Nawaz Jung played host to Rabindranath Tagore on his visit to the city. As a mark of respect for his distinguished service to the state and the country, he was conferred the *Padma Vibhushan* in 1965 - the highest civilian honour awarded by the Government of India.

Syed Ali Bilgrami

A remarkable academician and linguist, Syed Ali Bilgrami was an outstanding bureaucrat who served in the Nizam's Civil Service. As Director of Public Instruction, Home Secretary, Inspector General of Mines and Secretary Public Works Department, he made significant contribution to the city and the state. He was a fellow of the Geological Society of London and was a great scholar of Persian, Sanskrit and English. Syed Bilgrami was instrumental in establishing the Asifia Library.

Maqdoom Mohiuddin

Maqdoom Mohiuddin was one of the greatest Urdu poets of Hyderabad. A radical poet and activist, Maqdoom played many roles in his life time. As an active member of the Communist Party of India, his speeches and writings were fairly revolutionary and anti-government, for

Syed Ali Bilgrami

which he once served a prison term. In 1952, he was elected a member of the Lok Sabha.

Maqdoom's speeches were as fiery as his writing was compelling. He published his book on Tagore's poetry in 1935. In 1940, his collection of poems called '*Surkh Savera*' and in 1961, '*Gul-i-Tar*', were published. His poems were so popular that they were translated in not just other Indian languages but also Russian and German. He died in 1969 but his avant-garde verses keep him alive in the memories of his countless admirers.

Ali Yawar Jung

Mirza Ali Yawar Khan belonged to an illustrious family of Hyderabad. His father, Nawab Khedive Jung was a renowned doctor and his mother, Tyeba Begum, daughter of Nawab Imad-ul-Mulk, was a social activist.

Ali Yawar Jung studied in England and Paris and on his return, taught history at Osmania University. He later joined the Nizam's government and rose to become a Minister. Twice, he served as the Vice Chancellor of Osmania University. He represented India at the United Nations and served as the Indian Ambassador to Argentina, Egypt, Yugoslavia, France and the United States of America.

Nawab Saheb was appointed the Governor of Maharashtra in 1970. In 1976, while still in office, he passed away. The Government of India conferred the highest civilian awards, the *Padma Bhushan* and later the *Padma Vibhushan* on Nawab Ali Yawar Jung for his distinguished service to the nation.

Ronald Ross

Sir Ronald Ross was born in 1857 at Almora in the hills of Kumaon. He studied in England and pursued a degree in medicine there. In 1881, he returned to India and joined the British army as a medical officer. While stationed in Hyderabad, he identified the parasite responsible for the spread of Malaria – a dreaded disease that had killed many.

In 1902, Ronald Ross received the Nobel Prize for his research in the field of tropical medicine. The building where he lived and worked still exists in Begumpet, Hyderabad.

A painting of Princess Niloufer at Niloufer Hospital

PROFILES IN COURAGE

Beneath Hyderabad's affluent veneer was a dark crevice where women deprived of education and opportunities had been relegated to. Women in the nineteenth and early twentieth century Hyderabad, as in most parts of India, were confined to their homes with little aspirations and no dreams. However, there were a few remarkable women who were determined to change their world, educate and empower them.

Noorunnisa Begum, the daughter of Sir Salar Jung I was one such lady who was proficient in English, Persian, Urdu and Arabic and started a school, in the memory of her father. Hers was an elitist school that admitted girls from aristocratic families, where apart from learning, students were given lessons in etiquette.

In 1910, **Tayyaba Begum Sahiba Bilgrami** was the first Muslim lady in India to graduate from Madras University. A mother of five, she strove hard to educate women as she firmly believed that learning was the key to progress. Her speeches and writings dealt with Indian and Islamic sociological contexts pertaining mainly to women's issues. She worked with other women to provide relief to hundreds who were rendered homeless in the floods of 1908. She was instrumental in starting the Mahboobia Girls School, an elite public school for girls. She promoted arts, crafts and vocational courses for women and, as President of the *Anjuman-i-Khavatin-i-Islam*, guided a number of women to become financially independent.

Tyaba Baqar Ali Khan was another lady who strove relentlessly for the cause of women's education. In 1940, when Muslim women seldom stepped out of *Purdah*, she was bold enough to join the state government's cooperative department. She started the Arts and Crafts School and also the Domestic Science College for women in the city. Both the institutions were popular among women for they not only honed their home managerial skills, but also enabled them to seek jobs outside.

Sughra Humayun Mirza was a scholar and activist who took up the cause of educating Muslim women. Along with Tyeba Bilgrami she founded the *Anjuman-i-Khavatin-i-Islam*. She was a keen writer who contributed to magazines and newspapers and even authored books on issues like women's education, evils of *Purdah*, Hindu Muslim unity, ban on cow slaughter and need for national universities. In 1923, she was elected a

Mahalaqa Chanda Bai

member of the Royal Asiatic Society, London. She raised funds for Aligarh University and helped the victims of the Musi floods of 1908. She started a school for girls at Masab Tank.

Mahlaqa Chanda Bai was a celebrated dancer, singer and writer in the court of the second Nizam. One of the most beautiful women of her time, she was an accomplished poet and her *Ghazals* were often compared with the compositions of the gifted poet king Muhammad Quli Qutub Shah. She was the first to compose in the nascent *Dakhani* language and her poetry was appreciated in faraway cities like Delhi and Lucknow. After her death, an anthology of her work was published as *Gulzar-i-Mahalaqa*. The Nizam relied on her wisdom and permitted her to attend the *Durbar* to advise him on state policies. The area around Adikmet was gifted to her as a *Jagir* where Osmania University stands today.

The lady was a skilled rider and dressed as a man, would accompany the Nizam even to the battlefield. A sage, Qudratullah Qasim, described Mahalaqa Chanda Bai as a unique combination of body and soul.

Sarojini Naidu, popularly known as the Nightingale of India, was a celebrated poet and writer. India, at this time, was in the throes of the freedom struggle and Ms Naidu too joined it. She was a member of the Home Rule League delegation that went to England. She also attended the second Round Table Conference in London. She was a staunch advocate of Hindu Muslim unity and always propogated that India's strength lay in unity. At the Bombay Congress in 1915, she spoke in support of the resolution on Self Government. A close associate of Mahatma Gandhi and the Nehru family, she served as the Governor of United Province.

Sarojini Naidu

Princesses Niloufer and Durr-e-Shehvar, the two most beautiful women of Hyderabad were the daughters-in-law of the seventh Nizam, Mir Osman Ali Khan. Princess Durr-e-Shehvar, wife of the elder son, Prince Azam Jah Bahadur, was the daughter of Sultan Abdul Majeed, the last Caliph and former ruler of Turkey and Princess Niloufer wife of the younger prince, Moazzam Jah, was the niece of the Caliph. These two extremely beautiful and fashionable cousins completely dominated Hyderabad's social circles. Their beauty and charm along with their sense of fashion captivated the *Hyderabadis*.

Princess Niloufer and Princess Durr-e-Shehvar graced a number of forums and clubs and a large number of European women joined them. Princess Niloufer was also associated with the Red Cross and organizations concerned with children's health and welfare. Hyderabad's biggest children's hospital was named after her.

Princess Durr-e-Shehvar with her son Prince Mukarram

Princess Niloufer with staff members of Model Primary School, 1938

A RICH CULTURAL MOSAIC

The culturally rich Hyderabad had been nourished with care by the Asif Jahi rulers. The Hyderabadi society became a locus of great creative elegance, fashion, rituals and traditions that were drawn heavily from the grandeur and style of the great Mughals. Delhi was the spring from where new trends in style and fashion flowed, to be quickly absorbed by the echelons of the class-ridden Hyderabad society. This happy amalgamation of ethnic customs with Mughal traditions left a maelstrom of images in its wake, enthralling to watch and decipher.

Mir Mahboob Ali Khan, the sixth Nizam.

'Tehzeeb' or court etiquette

The first Nizam grew up inspired by Aurungzeb and it was on the lines of the rich Mughal tradition that he fashioned the protocol to be followed in the court and the royal palace. After assuming power in 1720, he brought about a sea change in the affairs of the state: the norms of working, official procedures and etiquette to be followed in the court.

Court Etiquette:

Anyone entering the court had to sign first. He was immediately briefed by the concerned officials about the protocol to be followed in the court. A headgear (*dastar*) and a belt (*buglus*) had to be worn over a long coat (*sherwani*). The headgear imitated the style prevalent in the court of the great Mughal Emperor, Akbar. The nobles were permitted to adorn themselves with jewellery only on special occasions and there was a restriction on the number of pieces they wore. Even the length of the fabric and the style of the dress of the nobility followed strict specifications.

A sword *(Dhup)* could be carried in the court but not a walking stick. With the exception of the security personnel on duty, no other individual was permitted to carry arms on person while entering the court. When the curtains were drawn in the personal chambers of the Nizam, even the servant carrying the smoking pipe *(Hukka)* or the wash basin was not allowed in. However, the messenger who carried news was allowed to communicate it directly to the Nizam. The writers who drafted the official documents and a personal attendant who carried the royal pen case *(Qalamdanbardar-i-khas)* formed a part of the Nizam's personal entourage.

The *durbar* or meetings lasted an hour and a half at the most and forty eight minutes at least. At the end of the stipulated time the officer on duty announced the wrapping up of the conference. Only the Principal Assistant or his deputy *(the Munib and the Peshkar)* could get papers signed by the Nizam. The first paper signed in the day had to be a document related to charity followed by others. Court etiquette established during the time of Nizam-ul-Mulk was followed by the other Nizams with little modifications.

In the *Durbar* (court) the Nizam sat cross legged on a marble seat over a Persian carpet. He would recline on a long bolster*(musnud)* covered in yellow satin. His sons would sit behind him. The

Personalized buckle with an etched image of Mahboob Ali Pasha, Asif Jah VI.

courtiers would then step up one by one with their right palm upturned and held over the left, to offer gold or silver coins wrapped in a white handkerchief to the Nizam. The Nizam would touch the offering (*nazar*) and pass it on to his assistant. After making the offering, the courtier had to bow and walk backwards towards his seat, as no one could show their back to the Nizam.

Wearing footwear in the *Durbar* was forbidden. The Prime Minister and the nobles sat barefoot on the carpet to the left of the throne, with their heads covered. When the British were visiting the Nizam they sat to his right, barefoot, but with their head uncovered. When one visiting Resident requested for a chair, Afzal-ud-Daula, the fifth Nizam, angrily snapped back, 'let a pit be dug under his feet.' During the time of Mahboob Ali Pasha, chairs were introduced much to the relief of the visiting foreign dignitaries. Mahboob Ali Pasha, the sixth Nizam changed the official language from Persian to a simpler Urdu, another import from the Mughal court.

The grandeur and splendour in the court never dimmed. By the twentieth century the celebrations at the court were more ostentatious than ever before.

A young Prince

Official attire of a Taluqdar, 1915

Homes and lifestyle of the aristocracy

The Hyderabad homes of this period were known as *deoris* wherein the living quarters of men and women were strictly segregated – the *zenana* for the women and a separate quarter or *mardana* for men with a corridor connecting the two parts of the house. A thick curtain called the *chilman* covered the door leading to the *zenana* and a woman sat there, loudly announcing the arrival of a visitor. Even husbands and sons could not enter the *zenana* unannounced. The house would have a central courtyard flanked by rooms on all sides and every room had a verandah in front which was called the *dalaan*.

The largest *dalaan* was the formal living room of the house. The living room had a *Takht* or a low settee draped with a gold embroidered velvet cover. Visitors would recline on *musnads* or bolsters placed on the settee. On a small stool a siver *paandaan* or a container for betel leaves, was placed. *Paan* or betel leaf was wrapped in silver foil or '*warq*', held together with a silver pin and served on a silver tray. On the side of the settee was placed a silver *hookah* or a smoking pipe which was passed around. Women, too, smoked the *hookah*. Rose water and *ittar* or perfume was sprinkled on guests to welcome them. Every respectable home had a collection of silver placed in the living room, comprising a container for rose water, *hookah*, *paandaan* and a spittoon.

Life in the *zenana* was full of activity with weddings, festivals, rituals and ceremonies to attend and dress up for. Any occasion was an excuse for festivity, fun and frolic. Games like chess, *kodi*, *Bait bazi* and *patang bazi* or kite flying kept the women entertained.

A child on a stroller. Pic: Raja Deen Dayal

Men's style of dressing

The official dress of the Prime Minister, approved by the Nizam

When it came to dressing, both men and women had an evolved sense of style. A popular dress of the royalty was the *Deccani Angarakha* a loose garment falling to the ankle and worn with a gold embroidered cap. Initially men wore a tunic inside the *Angarakha* which was later replaced by a shirt with cuffs and collar, an evident British influence. The *Neemjama*, a mughal dress was commonly worn in the Nizam's court. Made of fine muslin, hence light and flimsy, it was popular among both Muslims and Hindus.

During the reign of Mahboob Ali Khan, the sixth Nizam, we notice a remarkable change in the style of dressing. The *neemjama* which was the old mughal traditional costume with an overdress made of yards and yards of muslin, gave way to a more streamlined, long, high collared jacket called the *sherwani*, worn with a *churidar* or a *pyjama*. This, along with the belt *(buglus)* and the headgear *(dastar)* was the official dress to be worn in the presence of the Nizam. The religious saints *(Ulemas)* had the liberty to choose their own dress.

Salar Jung III dressed in a churidar, kurta and a fur trimmed short coat

Raja Balwant Bahadur of Amarchinta Samasthan, 1913

The Nizam's headgear *(dastar)* was a bright yellow and was adorned with a *turah*, a beautiful piece of jewellery made with gold thread. Only the Nizam and members of the royal family had the privilege to adorn their headgear with a *turah*. The chief nobles could wear head gears in different styles as per their family tradition, while those who had lost their father, wore only white *dastars*.

The Hindus wore *dhotis* (a long cloth wrapped around the lower half and then pleated and tucked at the back) with shirts and *kurtas*. *Sherwanis* and *pajamas* were equally popular among the Hindus. Fabric ranging from handloom to silk and expensive brocade woven with gold thread were used for the *sherwanis*. Osman Ali Khan, the seventh Nizam, wore the most inexpensive *sherwanis* with cotton socks and ordinary shoes bought locally . Salar Jung II wore handloom *sherwanis* to promote the local weavers. An English tailor in Secunderabad excelled in making special *sherwanis* where the fabric used was never repeated for any two customers. These hallmark dresses, though pretty expensive were popular among the elite. At the other end of the spectrum was a shop in Abids, where an entire outfit could be bought for six rupees!

Mahboob Ali Pasha, the sixth Nizam loved to dress well. His *sherwanis* were exquisite and so were his gold embroidered caps. His headgear or *dastar* was always adorned with *turah* – a gold ornament. Turkish caps or *topi* was another very popular feature of the attire. Caps became a style statement coming in different shapes and styles. In the early twentieth century, a new style of caps called the *balon ki topi* or caps with hair was popular. Started first by Moin-ud-Daula, a Paigah noble, it was soon adopted by Salar Jung II. In Hyderabad, it was fashionable to wear the cap at an angle, popularly known as *tirchi topi*. The footwear to go with the *sherwani* was *zeirpai, apashahis* or *salim shahi* shoes. Fancy footwear would be lined with velvet. The a*pashahi* slippers made of soft goat skin and lined with velvet were so soft that they could be folded and put away. Socks made a late entry, somewhere in the late nineteenth or twentieth century. The nobles kept long beard and moustache as per the Islamic tradition.

Carrying weapons was a sign of authority and the nobles proudly carried arms like the sword (*Talwar*) or smaller weapon called the *Katar* or *Khanjar* that hung at the waist.

A Hindu King

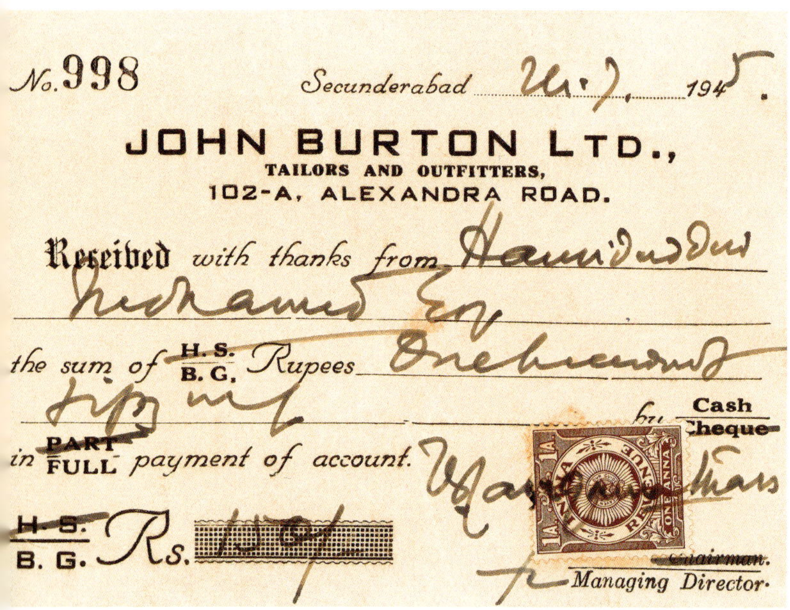

No. 998 Secunderabad .... 1945.

JOHN BURTON LTD.,
TAILORS AND OUTFITTERS,
102-A, ALEXANDRA ROAD.

Received with thanks from Hamiduddin Mohamed Esq
the sum of H.S. / B.G. Rupees One hundred fifty only
by Cash / Cheque
in PART / FULL payment of account.
H.S. / B.G. Rs. 150/-
Chairman.
Managing Director.

A receipt of John Burton, a famous English tailor and outfitter in Secunderabad, 1945

Raja Rayan Bahadur in all his regal finery, 1896

Fashion for women

A traditionally attired Hindu woman, 1880-85

Princess Durr-e-Shehwar with son Prince Mukharram Jah

The aristocratic women bathed in fragrant water everyday. On some days it was rose or jasmine flowers while on others it was *ittar* (perfume) and sometimes even milk. The lady attendant would then dry their hair with the heat of *Agar* or *Udh* (fragrant natural incense) burnt on charcoal in a small terracotta container. Hands and feet were anointed with henna for an attractive red colour. Hair was usually left long and plaited or wound in a bun called *juda* and strung with fresh flowers, very often jasmine. Tinkling glass bangles in myriad colours adorned their wrists. Women used kohl or *surma* for the eyes and liberally used *ittar* or locally made perfume. *Khus, gulab, motia* and *chameli* were the popular fragrances used according to the occasion, season and mood. A sprinkling of *afshan* and *chamki* or gold dust added glow to their face.

The Asif Jahi women keenly followed the current style and trends in fashion. Saree were popular and so was *Khada Dupatta* or a stole or a longish wrap worn over a loose kurta (shirt) or a *choli* (blouse) and a pyjama which was either left loose or tightly gathered at the ankle. The fabric used for the dresses ranged from simple cotton to heavy brocades with gold and silver embroidery. The *Dupatta* or stole could be *mulmul* (muslin) or heavy tissue or silk often embroidered in gold and silver. Hindu women, on the other hand preferred the nine yard saree with the pleats tucked behind. Unmarried girls wore the *lehenga* or a loose flowing skirt upto their ankle paired with a blouse and a *dupatta*. Flowers adorned their hair and they wore *bottu* or the vermillion mark on their forehead.

A famous singer Feroz Begum, 1885

Asif Jahi costumes on display at Chowmahalla

A PASSION FOR JEWELLERY

Anklets studded with pearls, diamond and rubies

Makers of gold and the makers of verse,
The twin creators that sway the world's secret desire for mystery,
Ah me! My heart outflows in tears,
And as the teardrop falls,
My lap is full of precious gems:
They're pearls and rubies all!
The makers of gold and the makers of verse,
The twin creators that sway the world's secret desire for mystery'.

– Osman Ali Khan, the seventh Nizam

The kingdom of the Asif Jahs encompassed the vast region of the Golconda mines and the rulers lived by the old tenet that the best and the most precious stones mined, went to the king. After the Mughals, the Asif Jahs were the biggest buyers of precious stones. The Mughal tradition of offering *Nazar* or gifts of diamond, gold and precious stones to the king was perpetuated by the Nizams. As a result, the nobles and the subjects outdid each other in offering bigger and costlier gems and jewels to the Nizams. The Nizam's jewellery chests were overflowing and it

A diamond and emerald studded sarpech

is said that at the time of the first Nizam's death in 1748, his wealth could easily sustain seven generations of the family.

A diamond necklace

In 1785, the second Nizam is said to have presented King George III with the hundred and one carat Hastings diamond. In 1799, the Nizam celebrated the fall of Seringapatnam by offering his own pearl necklace to the British Resident James Achilles Kirkpatrick. Mahboob Ali Pasha loved collecting precious stones and is said to have bought the exquisite and magnificent Jacob Diamond weighing a whopping 457.5 carats in the rough, from a dealer Alexander Malcolm Jacob. The transaction led to a criminal suit and the Nizam had to depose before a commission – an event marked with deep indignation and humiliation. Thereafter, the Nizam never cared much for this stone and it was chanced upon accidentally by his son, Osman Ali Khan in one of his father's shoes. The diamond now reduced to 184.5 carats and worth more than four hundred crore today, was later found on the seventh Nizam's desk wrapped in a rag being carelessly used as a paper weight.

Romance with Pearls

Hyderabad's romance with pearls is closely linked with the Nizam's great fondness for jewellery. These riches of the sea found a flourishing market in Hyderabad, a city not even remotely close to it. However, Hyderabad is strategically located roughly midway between two ports, Machlipatnam and Goa. Its location made it a bustling business center where diamonds, precious stones and pearls were traded. Another reason that made Hyderabad the city of pearls was the expertise that the local artisans had acquired in the delicate art of piercing and stringing pearls. Labour was cheap here and that made life easy for the traders who got most of their pearls from Basra, a city on the coast of the Persian Gulf.

All the seven Nizams and the members of their family owned enormous amounts of Basra pearls and jewellery, but it was Mir Osman Ali Khan, the seventh Nizam, who possessed the most incredible collection of pearls. Mounds of precious Basra pearls were routinely taken out in buckets, washed in water, sun dried on the terrace of the royal palace and stashed away. So much for maintenance!

Till today, Hyderabad remains the biggest market for pearls in India with more than four hundred shops in the city dealing only in pearls. Instead of Basra however, today pearls are sourced from China and Japan. India was also the biggest market for Colombian emeralds, and Burmese rubies.

A woman adorned from head to toe, 19th Century

Mahboob Ali Khan's daughter

That jewellery played a vital role in the lives of the Hyderabadis during the time of the Asif Jahs can be assessed by the fact that between 1891 and 1901 there were nearly two hundred thousand jewellers working in Hyderabad. During the reign of Nizam Ali Khan II, a permanent jewellery bazaar was set up at Shahi Julukhana in the city. A large number of jewellers set up shop between Gulzar Hauz and Charkaman. Anandi Ram, Komariji Naik and Hiralal Kanji were the important jewellers of Hyderabad.

Hyderabad during the Asif Jahs produced an incredible gamut of exquisite ornaments, second only to the Mughals. The Nizams' jewellery comprised a mind-blowing collection of *sarpech*, necklaces, belts, buckles, bracelets, bangles, earrings, armlets, toe rings, finger rings, pocket watches, chains, buttons and cufflinks and formed a very important component of the attire for both men and women. While styling the pieces, intricate floral patterns and elaborate setting of precious and semi precious stones in gold were used. *Kundan* or uncut diamonds combined with other precious and semi precious stones were set in gold. Another popular technique imported from Persia was '*Minakari*' where gold and silver jewellery was enameled in different colours and in different patterns. '*Navratna*' – or nine gems, wherein nine different precious stones were beautifully coordinated and set in gold was another popular style.

When it came to fashion and jewellery, the *Begums* or the ladies of the royal family were the trendsetters. The daughter of the sixth Nizam, Mahboob Ali Khan, wore the most beautiful pieces of jewellery. Her caps were studded with precious stones and her outfits embellished with pure gold thread.

Since the time of the QutubShahi rulers, Golconda had become an important center of diamond trade. In the city's Karwan area, a large number of diamond cutting and polishing units mushroomed.

Women adorned their forehead with *tikka* and *jhumar* while different styles of ear studs and ear rings called *anti, adraj, butte, jhumka, pankhe, phool baali, jhilmili, long ke phool, karn phool, chakriyan* and *awez* formed a part of the collection.

For the nose, rings in different styles called the *balq, biyasar, dal* and *nath* were worn. Necklaces had different names like *thassi, tulsi, champakali, chantak, chandanhar, sat-lada,*

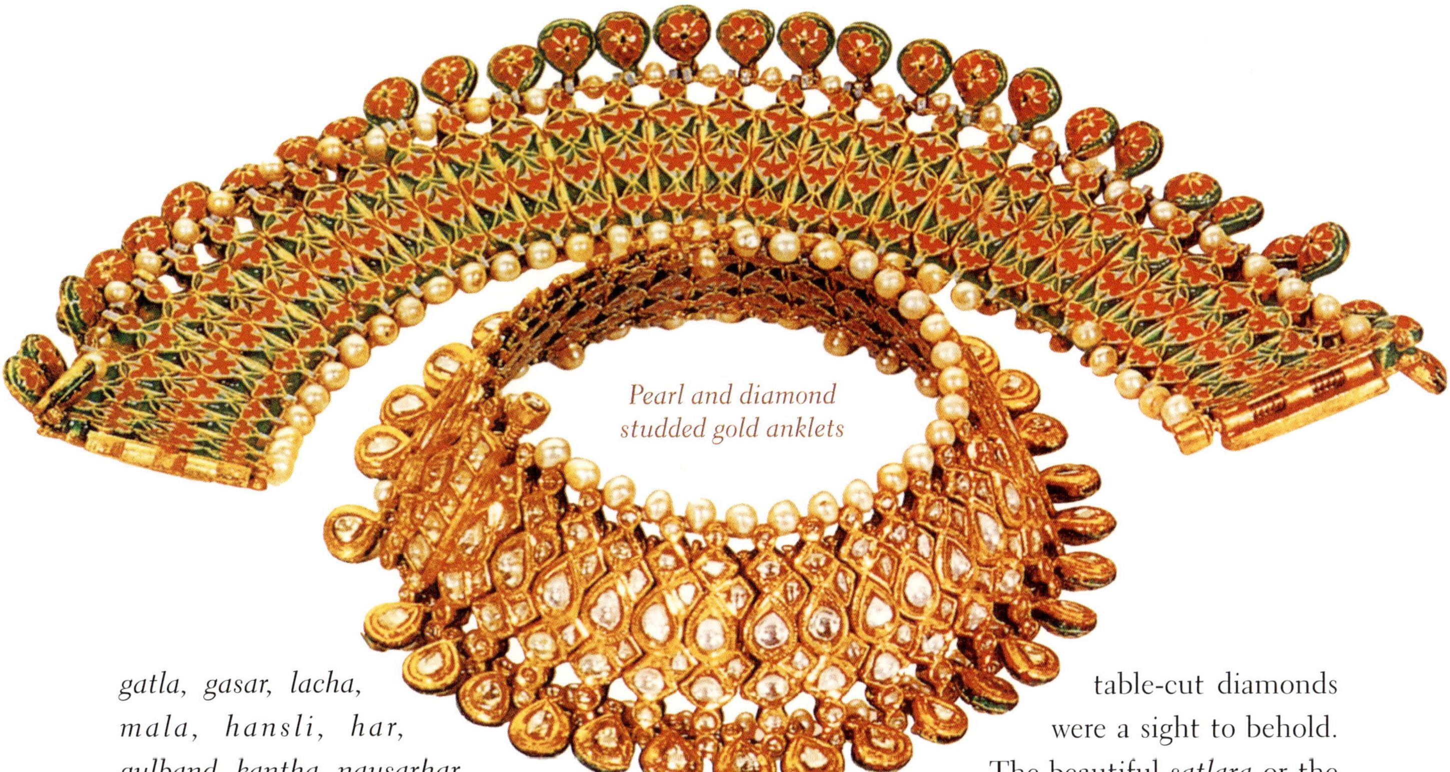

Pearl and diamond studded gold anklets

gatla, gasar, lacha, mala, hansli, har, gulband, kantha, nausarhar, hamail, badhi, taweez and *nadili*. A wide range of ornaments adorned the upper arm namely *bazooband, bazoo ke taweez, bazoo ke kade, kangini, nauratan, dand beech band, josh* and *dastband*. Bangles in different styles called the *panchi, kangan, goat, sumran, behar batwa, pariband, kade* and *arsi* adorned the wrists of the Asif Jahi women.

Waist bands in silver or gold called the *zar kamar* or *patta* were worn by the women and so were anklets of different styles called the *pazeb, tode, payal, ramjhul, gajreh, lol, kade* or *khal-khal*. Toe rings too had different names like *ghul, chutki* or *challa* .

The *sarapa* or jewellery from head to toe was a collection that included necklaces called the *kanthi, haar* and *mala*, armbands known locally as the *bazuband* and *bhujband* and bracelets called the *dastband* and *sumran*. These pieces could be worn individiually or together on special occasions to mark coronations, visits or any festive occasion. The necklaces with huge table-cut diamonds were a sight to behold. The beautiful *satlara* or the seven string pearl necklace with pendants was another exclusive piece of jewellery designed during the time of the Asif Jahs.

The courtesans and the dancing girls adorned chunky jewellery as is seen in the pictures of Mahlaqa Chanda Bai, a popular singer in the court of Nizam Ali Khan, Asif Jah II. She entertained Nawab Sikander Jah, Mir Alam and Raja Chandulal and loved to wear and flaunt heavy jewellery.

The Nizams themselves were extremely fond of jewellery and any occasion like coronations, weddings, birthdays, *Durbars*, visit of foreign dignitaries or just a whim warranted the purchase of yet another piece of fine jewellery. The Nizam would reward his nobles with a variety of ornaments which they would wear on special occasions or even to court. Mahboob Ali Pasha, the sixth Nizam rarely wore any jewellery as he preferred to dress in suits and western wear. The seventh Nizam, Osman Ali Khan, was a great connoisseur of good jewellery and commissioned the jewellery for his queens. Collecting jewellery specially rings studded with precious stones was his hobby.

The '*Sarpech*' was the proud ornament that adorned the headgear of the Nizams. After 1857, when Queen Victoria ascended the British throne, no Indian prince was allowed to wear a crown and that explains the emergence of *sarpech*, a head ornament that symbolized royalty. The *sarpech* comprised of a *sarpatti*, *jaigha*, *turrah* and the *kalghi* delicately strung together around the headgear. All the four pieces were embellished with table-cut diamonds and drops of emerald and pearls. The *kalghi* or the paisley shaped center-piece was the most flamboyant of the entire ensemble and was again studded with diamonds, pearls, rubies and emeralds. The back side of the ornament was enameled in red and green, in a classical Mughal style.

Nizam's jewellery collection displayed at the Salar Jung Museum

Sarpech – the proud ornament that symbolized royalty

Taking a cue from the royal family, the Salarjungs, the Paigah nobles and other *nawabs* and members of their family, wore heavy jewellery. An interesting fact was that many a time, valuable pieces were not even handed to the person for whom they were made. They were kept in the treasury and the treasurer kept a record of the number of times the pieces were taken out, worn, its condition and any special care it needed. At times, it was these treasurers who decided which ornament was to be worn and by whom on a special occasion. It was due to these stringent rules that they have survived for us to admire today.

After the merger of Hyderabad with the Union of India in 1948, Nizam Osman Ali Khan constituted a number of trusts, the most prominent of which were the HEH The Nizam's Jewellery trust and H.E.H The Nizam's Supplementary Jewellery Trust. In order to safeguard the precious bounty, all the Nizam's jewels were placed in the custody of these trusts whose trustees were the members of the royal family. The trust stipulated that the jewellery could not be sold until after the death of Osman Ali Khan and his elder son Prince Azam Jah. After Osman Ali Khans's death, an arduous legal wrangle ensued between the trustees and the Government of India over the custody of the Nizams jewels. In 1995, after twenty three years of litigation and a compensation of a whopping Rs 218 crore, the Government of India finally gained control over a part of the Nizam's jewels.

In 2001 the collection was exhibited for the first time at the National Museum in Delhi and later in the year at the Salar Jung Museum in Hyderabad where all caught a glimpse of the opulence and glory of a golden era now buried in layers of history.

CUISINE – A CAPTIVATING FARE

A tea party at the British Residency, 1945

Food during the time of the Nizams was a rich blend of Turkish, Afghani, Iranian, and Arabian cuisine evocatively blending the magic of oriental flavour with the earthy energy of ethnic cuisine. The nourishing romance between the two cultures created a very rich art of gastronomy that took several resonances signifying at once the rich culture of the region and a great tradition of hospitality.

Mealtime in a *Hyderabadi* home was not just a routine but a ritual, a time for celebration. A meal was the grand finale of a concerted effort since daybreak to give perfect flavour and taste to the well laid out spread of the day. No guest could leave a *Hyderabadi* home without sharing a meal with the family. In most aristocratic homes there were specialist cooks for meat dishes or desserts or the all time favourite – *Biryani*. While the male cooks were referred to as *Bawarchis*, the female cooks were affectionately called *Mamas*. The fondness of *Hyderabadis* for good food had turned quite a few of them into alchemists who magically transformed simple rice into exotic *biryani* and meat into delectable *kababs* and *qurmas*. One of General Raymond's French officers had this to write about *biryani*, 'rice boiled with quantities of butter, fowls and kids, with all sorts of spicery...... which we found to be very good, and which refreshed us greatly.' This was a dish entirely indigenous and had many variants *like Biryani Khaam, Biryani Zard or Zafrani* or the most exotic of all *Joban Malti Biryani* in which mutton, partridges and quails were cooked with rice.

Pathar ka gosht or marinated meat cubes cooked on hot stone was another delicacy of the area. So was *haleem* or minced meat cooked with butter and ground wheat. As Nawab Mahboob Alam Khan, an expert on *Hyderabadi* cuisine and a cook par excellence reminisces, *how* breakfast in an aristocratic home consisted of *khichdi, kheema, khagina* (egg and onion curry) along with *paratha* cooked in fresh home made butter. He adds that on festive occasions, breakfast comprised of *nahari, kulcha, zaban* and *paya* prepared with sheep and goat meat. On other days, the fare was vegetarian. *Baghare baingan* (spicy eggplant) *and mirchi ka saalan* (green chilli curry) were the popular vegetarian dishes of Hyderabad. Desserts like *double ka meetha* (bread pudding) or *khubani ka meetha* (apricot pudding) *or seviyon ka musafir* (vermicelli pudding) were relished here. Khan Saheb says, that most likely the recipe for the apricot pudding was imported from Turkey. An interesting array of bread was baked here like *naan, kulecha naan, kulcha, shirmal, baqar khani roti, mullah do pyaza ki roti* and *Bibi Marium ki roti* to name a few. *Nawab Saheb* laments that a lot of the recipes have lost their true flavour and the younger generation, fed on fast food, is not exposed to our rich culinary heritage.

Right from cooking to the presentation, *Hyderabadis* were connoisseurs. Not only the best condiments spiced the food, but the dishes were beautifully garnished, served in the best of china and laid out on fancily embroidered cloth called the *Dastar Khan*. Food was laid out on *Chowkis* or short tables just around one and a half to two feet high. The guests sat on the carpet around the table and enjoyed their meal. Even today, *Chowki* dinners are very popular in Hyderabad. The concept of high chairs and dining tables came much later with the British.

Visitors have chronicled at least a hundred variety of dishes commonly cooked during this time, along with seventy five types of confectionary and thirty three kinds of sauces and relish. The entire menu on a special occasion or festivals was known as *tora* and portions sent to friends and dear ones was called *hissa*. *Tora* usually comprised of *biryani* – a delicately spiced rice dish cooked with meat, *kabab* or roasted meat, *qurma* – a spicy vegetable or meat curry, *shirmal* or *naan* (bread), *kheer* – rice pudding along with *chutneys* and pickles.

Dinner was rounded off with betel leaf or *paan* . Betel leaf was carried with great fanfare in silver containers called *paandaan*. With great panache, the attendant would add *chuna* or white lime, *katha* or a vegetable extract, cardamom, clove, ground tobacco and even different kinds of fragrances to the leaf and fold it in a triangle. On special occasions, the leaf was embellished with edible silver foil and tucked with a silver pin. The serving of *Paan* implied the end of the meal and time for guests to depart.

The cooks at the royal kitchen churned out appetizing meals when members of the royal family, nobles and dignitaries visited the palace. When the King of England, the British Viceroy, Dukes of Austria and Russia and the *Rajas* of the various Indian states visited Hyderabad, special banquets were hosted in their honour. On special occasions, especially in the festive month of *Ramzan*, the gates of the royal palace were thrown open to the poor who thronged in thousands to sample the royal cuisine.

Ms Bilkis I Latif in her book, 'The essential Andhra Cookbook', describes how particular Nawab Salar Jung was about his food. On a normal day, a table for forty was laid out at his palace. The meal began with five to six western courses followed by five or six courses of *Hyderabadi* cuisine and then desserts and fruits. When he travelled to Bombay, the Nawab stayed at the exclusive Taj Mahal Hotel but his food was cooked by his chefs in the salon of his special train and delivered at the hotel.

Ms Latif refers to the growing English influence on the local palate by the late nineteenth century. In 1898, a dinner to celebrate the Nizam's birthday had the following dishes on its menu.

Potage aux quenelles and a la reine
Poisson entrée
Pigeon with green peas
Gelatine of duck with olive oil
Roast saddle of mutton
Truffled turkey
Mutton Mughlai
Pillaf with chicken curry
Marble gateau pudding
Strawberry icecream
Cheese and devilled biscuits
Coffee and petit four

In January 1922 when the Prince of Wales visited Hyderabad, a state banquet was held at Chowmahalla Palace. The whole palace was decorated beautifully. The menu for the royal dinner read as follows:

Fortue clavie
Soles Richelieu
Mousse Strasbourgeosie
Selle de Pre Sale

A Chowki dinner
at the Qutub Shahi tombs

Dindinneau truffe
Asperges Glaces Se Gribiche
Peches Reine Margot
Dessert
Café

The guests were offered *attar*, a local perfume and *paan*, betel leaf, before they left.

Another notable component of *Hyderabadi* cuisine was a variety of fruits that was relished here. When the Arabs moved into the city they started growing pomegranates, guavas and figs in the orchards at Barkas – the neighborhood where they chose to reside. These fruits along with bananas, papayas, *sitaphal* and different kinds of berries were savoured by the locals. Even today, the city probably has the largest number of fruit markets in the country. Come summer and mangoes swamped the market and homes. Every home had a special room to store them. A servant was assigned the job of picking the ripe fruits, cleaning them and bringing them to the table. *Hyderabadis* claim that their mangoes are the best be it *Himayat, Benishan, Malgoba, Jehangir, Chima* or *Gulabi*.

It would be unfair to round off this chapter without mentioning the famous Irani Cafes of the city. These cafes, locally known as 'caifs', and their famous *Irani Chai* or tea served with a platter of Osmania biscuits, *Dil Khush* – a sliced bun with cream and cherry filling, tie biscuits and *Dil Pasand* a hard bun with a cherry and coconut filling are as integral a part of the *Hyderabadi* way of life as the *Biryani*, Charminar and the Golconda. In the seventeenth century during the Qutub Shahi regime, Persian traders came to India and brought the tradition of Irani cafes to the city. It was here that men preferred to spend a good part of their day catching up with friends as they relished their endless cups of tea. Due to the colonial influence around the cantonment, most cafes in Secunderabad had English names while cafes in Hyderabad, stuck to the traditional Urdu names. Thus we have the famous Paradise, Persis, Embassy, Astoria, Garden and Alpha cafes in Secunderabad and *Niagara, Zubeida, Madina, Shadaab, Savera* in Hyderabad. You would be surprised to know that the tradition is still broadly maintained!

Organizing lavish banquets was a matter of pride for the rulers and the aristocrats. They vied to outdo each other because the more impressive the spread, the more respect they garnered in the social milieu. The Nizams successfully set a rich tradition of festivity and feasting – a ritual that has become a *Hyderabadi* way of life where zest for life is intimately linked with passion for food!

Dinner at Nawab Mahboob Alam Khan's home

ROMANCE WITH URDU

Mir Mahboob Ali Khan,
the sixth Nizam was a gifted poet

The Nizams were great patrons of art and literature and Urdu was the favoured language in the court. Poetry became the key instrument of literary expression and a number of Nizams, their nobles and Diwans composed verses in Urdu. The language was significantly enriched by the contributions made by such literateurs as Mir Mahboob Ali Khan, Asif Jah VI and Mir Osman Ali Khan, Asif Jah VII.

In the twentieth century, Hyderabad witnessed a scholarly revival due to the efforts of Mahboob Ali Pasha and Osman Ali Khan. Mir Mahboob Ali Khan, the sixth Nizam wrote under the pseudonym Asif and was a great admirer of the renowned poet Mirza Khan Dagh. His poems dealt with serious social issues like education, the armed forces, moral values and civic matters. He would spontaneously break into poetry and very often addressed his subjects in verse.

Osman Ali Khan, the seventh Nizam was fluent in Arabic, Persian and Urdu and was a gifted poet as well. His Persian *ghazals* were known for their poignant grace, deep sensitivity and a keen observation of human behaviour and relationships. One of his *ghazals* translated into English by Sir Nazamat Jung reads as follows:

In my life I am the measure
Of the truth affection lends:
I'm on earth a test and trial
Of the vaunted faith of friends.

I'm the melody of sorrow
In the heart of silence born:
I'm the dirge's mournful wailing
O'er some wretch's grave forlorn.

When from life I've vanished nameless,
Thus the simple tale relates:
Osman proved the spite of fortune,
And the tyranny of faith.

Taking a cue from the Nizams, the nobles too indulged in poetry and came up with some splendid works in Urdu and Persian. Raja Kishen Pershad, Sir Nizamat Jung, Shaheed Yar Jung, Aziz Jung and Prince Moazzam Jah were the other eminent poets of the time. Hali, Sarshar, Iqbal, Fani, Asghar Josh, Hafiz and Jigar were poets who visited the court and left behind a precious legacy of Urdu literature. Daag Dehalvi, Ameer Minai, Josh Malihabadi, Fani Badayuni, Fasahat Jung 'Jaleel' and Yagana Changezi were illustrious Urdu poets who charged the literary air of Hyderabad.

Osman Ali Khan, the seventh Nizam

A large number of Hindu nobles were scholars of Urdu and Persian, the most notable of whom was Raja Kishen Pershad. He composed '*ghazals*' and poetry in Urdu under the pen name 'Shad'.

After the coming of Osmania University with Urdu as the medium of instruction, the language gained wider acceptance and Hyderabad became a great center of Urdu learning. A society called *Anjuman Taraq-i-Urdu* was founded under the guidance of the great scholar Maulvi Abdul Haq, fondly called 'Baba-i-Urdu' for expanding the scope of the language. From the thirty's to the sixty's, Urdu blossomed in the city as *mehfils* and *mushairas* or soirees were a regular feature not only amongst the aristocracy but also in middle class homes. Urdu poetry took the form of *ghazals* which were popularly recited and sung. Gifted writers like Makhdoom, Khurshid Ahmed Jami, Shaaz, Shahid Siddiqui and Sulaiman Areeb strode the literary scene of Hyderabad. Makhdoom's '*Jung-i-Azadi*', '*Intezar*', and '*Chand Taron ka Ban*' espoused the rich cultural sensitivity of the city and the people.

Locally, the language spoken was Dakhani, a local variant of Urdu. Delightfully creative and gentle, the *Hyderabadis* spoke the language with a sense of pride. The purists may scorn at the colloquial twist given to Urdu, but the *Hyderabadis* love their Dakhani. Though Urdu is the preferred language of the elite, it is hard to keep Dakhani out of a *Hyderabadi*. An interesting anecdote lays bare the strong affiliation of a *Hyderabadi* with Dakhani.

Does this street lead to Charminar?' a tourist asked a boy standing near a tea stall.
'*Hau*', replied the teenager nonchalantly. *Hau* is yes in Dakhani. A gentleman sipping tea at the stall rebuked the boy for using the word *Hau* and asked him to say '*Ji haan*' instead, which means the same in Urdu but sounds more dignified.

Mirza Khan Dagh,
a renowned Urdu poet of the time

Raja Kishen Pershad, a noted Urdu poet and calligraphist wrote under the pseudonym Shad

'Why, does *Hau* sound rude?' asked the puzzled teenager. '*Hau*,' replied the gentleman inadvertently!

Nawab Imad-ul-Mulk, Sir Nizamat Jung and the illustrious Sarojini Naidu, fondly christened the 'Nightingale of India' were the eminent English scholars of this era. Her famous work 'Nightfall in the city of Hyderabad' is a lustrous tribute to the city.

See how the speckled sky burns like a pigeon's throat, Jewelled with embers of opal and peridote.

See the white river that flashes and scintillates,
Curved like a tusk from the mouth of the city's gates.

Hark, from the minaret, how the muezzin's call,
Floats like a battle flag over the city wall.

From trellised balconies, languid and luminous
Faces gleam, veiled in splendour voluminous.

Round the high Charminar sounds of gay cavalcades, Blend with the music of cymbals and serenades.

Over the city bridge night comes majestical,
Borne like a queen to a sumptuous festival.

Dr Zore Abadiyat-i-Urdu group with Ms Sarojini Naidu, 1941

Ganesh idol in the City

FESTIVALS CALL FOR CELEBRATIONS

The Asif Jah rulers were extremely tolerant and both Muslim and Hindu festivals were celebrated with equal fervour in Hyderabad. While the Muslim festivals of *Id-ul-Fitr, Id-ul-Idha, Shab-i-Qadr, Shab-i-Barat, Shab-i-Miraj*, etc were celebrated with fanfare, the Hindu festivals like *Ugadi, Dussehra, Holi, Diwali, Janmashtami, Ganesh Chaturthi*, solar and lunar eclipses called for celebration and rejoicing and the the Nizam's government permitted the offices to close down after noon on certain festive days.

Christians celebrated Christmas, New Year, Good Friday and Easter and the Parsis celebrated *Navroz* with great enthusiasm. The ruling Nizam's birthday, Queen Victoria's birthday and even the King of England's birthday were occasions to celebrate in Hyderabad.

Ganesh Chaturthi

Ganesh Chaturthi marks the birth of Lord Ganesha, the remover of obstacles and harbinger of peace and prosperity, in every Hindu household. This festival was begun by Shivaji, the great *Maratha* warrior in Maharashtra and revived by Bal Gangadhar Tilak during India's struggle for independence. It was intended to revive patriotic spirit among the Indians and unite them in their struggle against the British .

Though Ganesh Chaturthi began in Maharashtra it soon spread to all the adjoining states specially Hyderabad. Idols of Lord Ganesha were installed and after ten days of festivity, were immersed in water. Even today, Hyderabad celebrates the festival with great passion and fervour. The biggest idol in the country is put up at Khairatabad and is usually more than thirty feet tall.

The Pothrajus dancing during Bonalu festivity

The spirit of revelry

Bonalu

Bonalu is another festival of Telengana with a distinct ethnic origin. In 1813, an epidemic broke out in Ujjain in Madhya Pradesh. The villagers believed that *Mahankali* or Mother Goddess was angry with the people and that had led to the outbreak of the epidemic. A *Hyderabadi*, who was serving in the army there, prayed to *Mahankali* and promised that if he survived the plague, he would build a *Mahankali* temple in Hyderabad. He did survive and on his return built the temple for the goddess at Secunderabad.

The *Mahankali Jatara* is still popularly celebrated in Hyderabad. This eleven day festival is celebrated in nearly sixteen hundred Devi temples in the city, the most popular being the two hundred year old *Mahankali* temple at Secunderabad. On the final day of the *Jatara* a ceremony called *Rangam* is performed where a young girl in a trance, believed to be blessed by the Goddess, predicts the future.

Dussehra

Dussehra is another important festival of the Hindus signifying the triumph of good over evil. Goddess Durga is worshipped for nine days and on the tenth day or Dussehra we celebrate the killing of Ravana, the demon king by Lord Rama. In Hyderabad Dussehra is associated with the festival of Bathkamma – a colourful floral festival where women dressed in all their finery arrange flowers in colourful pyramids and worship the local deity Bathkamma.

Ugadi

Ugadi is celebrated at the onset of spring as the Telugu New Year. The day marks the beginning of the Hindu lunar calender and it is believed that Lord Brahma, the creator of the Hindu pantheon started creation on this day. Spring is the season that heralds new beginnings and on this day, new neem leaves, raw mangoes and fresh jaggery is used to make the Ugadi *Pachadi* - a relish that is a must-have on this day. The sweet, sour and bitter taste of the *pachadi* is a reflection of life and its different flavours.

Sankranthi

Celebrated on the 14th of January every year, Sankranthi, the harvest festival, is the most important Hindu festival in this part of the country. It spreads over three days and farmers celebrate the harvesting of rice and other fresh crops. It is considered auspicious to take a holy dip in a river and worship the sun on this day. Decorative patterns or *muggu* is traced infront of every home. Freshly harvested rice, fresh jaggery and castor is used to make the savouries that people enjoy with their friends and family.

A muggu pattern

Ramzan

The holy month of *Ramzan* is very auspicious for the Muslims the world over and is an occasion for expression of goodwill and friendship. *Eid* is celebrated on the first day of *Shawaal*, the tenth lunar month of the Islamic calender immediately after *Ramzan*. Ramzan means the festival of breaking the fast and Muslims fast for thirty days before the festival. It is believed that the holy Quran came into existence during this month. *Sheerkurma* is the special dessert made on this day.

The Ramzan Namaz near Charminar

Muharram procession

Muharram

A large number of Muslims participate in the Muharram procession, the day of mourning commemorating the martyrdom of Hussain, the grandson of the Prophet, at the battle of Karbala. While mourning the death of Hussain, pious Shia men beat their chests and flagellate themselves creating devotional hysteria. When new moon is sited at Muharram, *Alams* (banners) are placed for public viewing at all the *Ashur Khanas* or the mourning halls. Though they do not join in the actual mourning, the Hindus accompany their Muslim compatriots to the mourning halls *(Ashurkhanas)*. These *Alams* are essentially the replicas of the banners carried by Imam Hussain at Karbala. Different *Alams* are taken out in processions on different dates of which *Bibi Ka Alam* taken out on the tenth day of Muharram has the most impressive attendance. The tradition of Bibi-ka-Alam dates back to the Qutub Shahi times.

Women watch the Moharram procession

Urs and Melas

The *Urs* or the anniversaries of holy men were occasions when Muslims and Hindus actively participated in the festivity. These fairs were annual events where people gathered to feast and celebrate with friends and family.

The important *Urs* were those of *Maula Ali*, *Baba Sherfuddin* of *Pahadi Sharif*, *Abdul Faiz at Bidar*, and *Hazrat Jehangir Peeran* near Hyderabad. Despite its Shia inspiration, the *Urs* at *Maula Ali* became a great center of devotion for Sufis, mystics and ascetics. From the 1780's onwards, due to the Nizams patronage, the *Urs* at *Maula Ali* became a popular destination for all – high and low, Hindus and Muslims, locals or visitors.

Chilla or the naming ceremony

On the fortieth day after birth, in a grand ceremony called *Chilla*, the new born was christened. When the child was four years, four months and four days old, the *Rasm-e-Bismillah* was performed where amidst the recital of Koranic verses the child was given a slate, a silver pen, an inkpot and a copy of the first chapter of the Koran. The child, dressed like a young prince, was then initiated by a family elder. He would make the child hold a pen and write the holy prayer, *Bismillah-Hir-Rahman-Nir-Rahim*. (I begin in the name of God, the most Merciful and Forgiving). Later, during the holy month of Ramzan when the child observed a day of fasting for the first time, family members celebrated the occasion as *Roza Kushai*.

Bismillah ceremony of Mirza Muhammed Ali Baig, November, 1904

Weddings

Weddings are the most important of all celebrations in Hyderabad. Right from the engagement to the wedding, households bustle with activity.

Professional women matchmakers were always on the lookout for an eligible bride or groom. These extremely tactful women would make

A wedding in 1891

note of their looks, family and financial status. They would then present an attractive package – a wee bit overstated as the need be, to the prospective bride or groom's family. Once both the families approved of each other, the wedding was fixed. A formal engagement or *Mangni* followed when the boy's family carried a gold ring, flowers, sweets and clothes for the bride.

The process of putting together the bride's trousseau began months in advance. Ceremonies like *Manjha*, *Sanchaq* and *Mehendi* preceded the *Nikah* or the wedding.

A Hindu wedding

A wedding on April 7th, 1886

A wedding in 1891

Dancers and singers at a wedding, 1870-75

Nawab Shah Alam Khan's grand childrens wedding, 2005

A Hindu wedding

The *qazi* (priest) solemnized the wedding in accordance with the Muslim Law. The *nikah* was a formal event and a *mehar* (alimony) was fixed and announced by the *Qazi* during the proceedings. The bride and groom saw each other for the first time in a mirror placed over the Holy Quran and before looking at the girl the groom recited *Sura Akhlas* from the Quran.

After the wedding, a grand feast called *Chauthi* was organized at the bride's home. The following day, on the occasion of *Walima*, the groom's family hosted an equally lavish banquet for friends and family.

A beautiful Hyderabadi bride

CRAFTS OF HYDERABAD

Bidri

The technique of Bidri craft is said to have travelled to India from Iran. The followers of Khwaja Moinuddin Chishti, a *sufi* saint who migrated to Ajmer in Rajasthan introduced this craft in India. In the fifteenth century, craftsmen travelled to modern day Karnataka and settled in Bidar from where it derived its name – Bidri. From Bidar some of the artisans migrated to Hyderabad making the city home to a highly skilled artform that thrived from the sixteenth to the nineteenth century. Although the artisans were not of Mughal descent, the art catered to the Mughal court and hence the floral motifs and embellishments has a distinct Mughal essence. However, the art form survived due to the unstinted support and patronage of the Nizams of Hyderabad.

In Bidri, a piece was first modelled on a lathe and the surface was then smeared with a solution of copper sulphate. The artist carved a motif and inserted thin wires of silver, brass or even gold into the chiseled outline. The object was treated with a paste of mud, ammonium chloride and other chemicals. The surface was now polished with oil and charcoal powder and rubbed vigorously to give it a sheen. The patterns usually chosen by the artisans were flowers, vines, animals, landscapes, geometric designs and calligraphy. Bidri was used mainly on *hookah* bases, ewers, boxes and buttons.

Today more contemporary motifs have been added to the repertoire to cater to international market. Hyderabad continues to be a flourishing center for this indigenous and exotic craft.

Calligraphy

Calligraphy was given the status of a divine art form during both the Qutub Shahi and the Asif Jahi times in Hyderabad and the Holy Quran, the laws of jurisprudence, royal *farmans* (announcements) and administrative writings were recorded beautifully. Hyder Khan, a noted calligrapher of the Asif Jah period produced copies of the Quran that were as good as the works of the Mughal and the Qutub Shahi periods. Displayed in the Salar Jung Museum is an amazing collection of calligraphy done during the Asif Jahi period including the works of Maharaja Kishen Pershad. The *Alams* or the shimmering standards cast in gold and silver taken out in the Muharram procession, consisted of stunning pieces of calligraphy. The names of the beloved five or *Panjatan* namely Muhammad, Ali, Fatima, Hussain and Hasan were beautifully inscribed on these *Alams*.

Silver Filigree

Nearly two centuries ago, the craft of silver Filigree was introduced in Karimnagar, a township 150 kilometers away from Hyderabad. Artisans in the village worked with pure silver wires of different gauge to create delicately carved boxes, trays, bangles, plates and perfume containers among other objects. The art was patronized by the Nizams and the Nawabs as it was a tradition in the aristocratic homes to gift kilos of attractive silver articles to the daughters for their wedding. After the reign of Osman Ali Khan, the last Nizam, this craft suffered a setback largely because it

lost its royal patrons and also because silver became expensive and artisans preferred to work on gold which had a bigger market.

Paintings

Paintings got a fresh lease of life during the reign of the Asif Jah rulers. Painters usually tapped the erotic pulse of the women of the times, depicting them in a state of aesthetic bliss. Women were the most preferred subject followed by portraits of rulers, saints, nobles, weddings and hunting processions. As most of the nobles in the nineteenth and early twentieth century were exposed to the outside world, it became fashionable to collect art specially paintings by European artists. By the end of the nineteenth century, the quality of the paintings began to deteriorate and the final nail was struck with the advent of photography in 1880. Photography completely dislodged this traditional art form and the precision and clarity of the pictures taken by Raja Deen Dayal had the *Hyderabadis* spellbound.

European paintings at Salarjung Museum

NATURE'S OWN CANVAS – THE ROCKSCAPE OF HYDERABAD

The afternoon sun peeks from behind the jagged silhouette of the rocks that hem the city and the expanse before me reaches out to the huge rocks in unusual shapes at the far end. These rocks, you would be surprised to know are older than the Grand Canyon and even the Himalayas!

A part of the Indian Peninsular Gneissic, these rocks spread over modern day Andhra Pradesh, Karnataka and Madhya Pradesh. During the course of the earth's rotation millions of years ago, the hot molten crust below spiralled out on the surface and cooled down taking unusual shapes. Gradually, these craggy unbalanced rock formations weathered and settled into a picturesque harmony, while the city grew around them. Precariously perched but perfectly balanced, these silent contorted layers of rock reveal a fascinating geological profile of the earth. They are nature's monuments and are more beautiful than all the man made relics in the city. Gunther Grass, a Nobel laureate and German litterateur who visited the city in 1986, was so fascinated by these oddly shaped rocks that he preferred to explore them rather than the usual tourist destinations in the city. He spent hours drawing pictures of the fascinating rocks all around, but lamented the indiscriminate quarrying that would ultimately destroy these nature's artifacts.

Rabindranath Tagore was so enthralled by the rocks of Hyderabad, that he penned a beautiful poem on them:

From the distance thou didst appear
Barricaded in rocky aloofness.
Timidly I crossed the rugged path
To find here all of a sudden
An open invitation in the sky
And a friend's embrace in the air.
In an unknown land the voice that
Seemed ever known
Revealed to me a shelter of loving intimacy.

These rocks provide natural drainage for the area and also serve as good aquifers. Aided by the water bodies in the region, they augment the irrigation requirements of the surrounding area.

In 2002, the Society to Save Rocks surveyed the rocks in and around Hyderabad and identified two hundred and fifteen species of avis, twenty four mammals, twenty seven amphibia and reptiles and eleven species of carnivores, thriving amidst the rocks. The team also noticed the presence of over ninety species of birds, both local and migrant, breeding in and around these rocks. The bio-diversity at hand is truly amazing!

In the race for quick expansion, the rocks of Hyderabad were the first casualty. They were incessantly destroyed to make way for new faceless structures that now blotch the city scape. This was a major setback for all the rock lovers, as Hyderabad is not only losing its charm but also its character. Little do these predators realize that buildings can come and go, but these rocks once gone shall never come back. In 1996, a group of rock lovers formed the 'Society to Save Rocks' to create awareness about the rocks and save them from extinction. On the recommendation of the society, the state government initiated action to save this priceless heritage and entrusted the Hyderabad Urban Development Authority Zoning Regulation with the task of guarding nine rock formations in and around Hyderabad as protected heritage precincts.

Gerard Hopkins had once asked, 'what would the world be, once bereft of wet and wilderness?' The truth is, there is no life beyond nature and destroying nature is destroying life.

HYDERABAD TO CYBERABAD

From a laid back leisurely Hyderabad to a cool and flamboyant Cyberabad, the city has come a long way. In the last decade, when information technology strode the world and the internet magically transformed lives, Hyderabad changed. Wired and networked, this was one Indian city looking and thinking differently. The splendid city of yore presented a stunning synergy of the old and the new and became a touchstone of progress and expansion!

Cyber Towers

Industrialization sets in

How did the city reinvent itself? The seeds of change were sown in the 1940's when Osman Ali Khan, the seventh Nizam, ordered the setting up of the Industrial Trust Fund which aided the setting up of a number of factories in the city, opening new vistas of growth and advancement. The sixth and the seventh decade saw the city transform into a magnet for industrial activity as several private and public sector enterprises mushroomed in and around the city. The coming of BHEL Bharat Heavy Electricals Limited and ECIL Electronics Corporation of India Limited stimulated the industrial growth of the city. Large industrial units came up in areas like Nacharam, Jeedimetla, Ramanthapur, Balanagar, Azamabad, Katedan, Moulali, Uppal, Cherlapalli, Patancheru, Bollaram and Saroornagar. Today, major companies like Satyam Computers, Dr Reddy's Laboratories, Aurobindo Pharma, IVRCL, Shantha Biotech, Apollo Hospitals, LANCO, GVK Industries, Nagarjuna Constructions, ITC and Andhra Sugars have made Andhra Pradesh the most industrial and investment friendly state in the country.

As the city triumphed over the perils of fast growth, it witnessed large scale migration from all over the country. According to the 2001 census, the population of Hyderabad Urban Agglomeration stands at 5.7 million and the decennial population growth from 1991 - 2001 has been 27.37%. People from far off Kashmir to Kerala chose to make Hyderabad their home. Relocation is not a new phenomenon in Hyderabad. Ever since the time of the Nizams, more than two hundred years ago, Hyderabad has witnessed large scale migration of Kayastha families from Uttar Pradesh and Parsis from Bombay. Later in 1956, when the state of Andhra Pradesh was formed, a sizeable population from the coastal areas of Andhra, Telengana and the Rayalseema region of the state moved into the city. Poverty and vagaries of nature, illiteracy and the apathetic growth of rural Andhra especially the Telengana region is responsible for the large scale migration to the city. Today however, the affluent upper and middle class populace is moving to the city due to better educational institutions, job opportunities and civic amenities available in the city. The city is easy to live in and the *Hyderabadis* are very tolerant and accepting of different cultures, languages and traditions. A guest is always welcomed with great trust and warmth in this city of the *Nawabs*. Language is not a deterrent unlike other southern cities as 'Dakhani', the language spoken here, is easily understood by all. Another major attraction is the moderate climate which is dry and breezy throughout the year.

However, the migrant's preference for the northern parts of the city over the southern end comprising largely of the old city, is due to the apathy towards the historic core of the city, the deficient civic amenities in the area and the already thick population there.This trend has greatly impacted the balance in the location of functional areas and the pattern of distribution of population in the entire city.

Today the Hyderabad metropolitan area spreads over 1905.04 square kilometers which is much more than the Hyderabad Census Agglomeration of 2001 which was approximately 778 square kilometers. This figure amply reflects the remarkable suburban growth around the city. The rapid expansion and industrial growth along with the boom in the IT industry, has resulted in skyrocketing land prices in the last decade. Property in the upmarket Banjara and Jubilee Hills, command unprecedented rates today, comparable maybe only to Bombay, Bangalore and Delhi.

'*Irani Café to Cyber Café*'

– an astounding makeover

Bill Gates in the city

From 'Irani Cafes to Cyber Cafés' - the makeover has been phenomenal! Till about two decades ago, the city had a languid pace where there was enough time to chat and exchange notes over endless cups of *masala chai* or spicy tea at the neighbouring Irani café. A *Hyderabadi's* sense of time was proverbial with the word '*parsoon*' or the day before yesterday, meaning any day between two days to two years ago. But in the last decade the attitude of the people has undergone a dramatic change.

Hyderabad's tryst with Information Technology started in the early ninety's when it became an incubator of the high-tech revolution that took the country by storm. When the IT fire engulfed the nation, it was stoked the most in Hyderabad. IT was the new *mantra* that stirred an entire generation to brace itself with a degree in computers as every career path now led to Silicon Valley or the plush workplace in the Hi Tec City – a new conglomerate of corporate offices that became the quintessence of Hyderabad's new *avtaar* as Cyberabad. The city emerged as a major base for global R&D centers, software development and Business Process Outsourcing (BPO). The destiny of the new techno savvy India was being rewritten on the

laptops of the young software professionals in the high tech offices of Madhapur.

The city's apt renaming brought it global attention. From Bill Clinton, Tony Blair to Bill Gates and George Bush, the city was every visiting dignitary's new whistlestop destination! A shining showcase of New India with software parks, call centers and internet cafes, Hyderabad was the perfect package to present, globally. Government lured and successfully roped in several multi-national companies and global giants like Microsoft, IBM, Oracle, Dell, Computer Associates, Motorola, GE Capital, HSBC, Google, Deloitte, Vanenberg, Intergraph, Infosys, Wipro, Mindtree Consulting and many more to set up offices in the city. Satyam Computer Services, a city based company has done phenomenally well and is a leading global software solution provider. Thanks to the healthy investment climate in the state Infosys is also looking towards a major expansion in Hyderabad.

For every contingency the city was ready with an option. The turn of the century added a new facet to the IT sector with multinational companies outsourcing work from India. Hyderabad saw the burgeoning growth of ITeS or IT-enabled services. Thanks to a large skilled workforce, low operational overheads, good infrastructure and a proactive government policy, the city today stands on the threshold of an ITeS revolution. In November 2004, software major, Microsoft opened a product development unit in Hyderabad – its second development center and also the biggest facility outside the US.

Bill Clinton on his visit to Hyderabad

British Prime Minister Tony Blair and his wife Cherie Blair interacting with children in Hyderabad

George Bush holds a pumpkin

Pharmaceutical hotspot

Aptly called the 'Bulk Drug Capital of India', Hyderabad dominates the country's pharmaceutical industry, contributing 33% of the bulk drugs produced in India. With an expertise in chemical synthesis, formulation and process engineering, the city has emerged as a pioneer in the pharma and biotechnology sector. The pharma industry of Andhra Pradesh is worth US $1.6 billion today and aims at reaching a figure of fifteen to twenty billion dollars by the year 2020. Along with the gaint Dr. Reddy's Laboratory, many other companies like Divi's, Matrix, Suven, Natco among others have given Hyderabad a strong and aggressive presence in the sector through product diversification, research and development, technology upgradation and high standard output.

Hyderabad always had a distinct lead over other cities due to the presence of IDPL (Indian Drugs and Pharmaceuticals Limited) and a well established R&D facility provided by institutions like Indian Institute of Chemical Technology (IICT), The Centre for Cellular and Molecular Biology (CCMB), Centre for DNA Fingerprinting & Diagnostics (CDFD) and National Institute of Nutrition (NIN).

World Class Health Care

Hyderabad has come of age in the field of health care and emerged as a major health care destination in India. A large number of corporate hospitals like L.V.Prasad Eye Institute, Apollo, CARE, Global Hospital, Medwin, Medi-Citi, CDR, Indo-American Cancer Hospital, Mullapudi Cardiac Center, Kamineni and KIMS among others provide world class multi-disciplinary healthcare and along with the Government hospitals which are being upgraded, aim to provide quality and affordable health care to all.

The Nizam Institute of Medical Sciences

Biotechnology – a major step forward

A scientist at work

With the strides made in the field of health care, education and research another region that has witnessed unprecedented growth is biotechnology. The turn of the century saw Hyderabad sell itself not just as an IT destination but also a frontrunner in the biotechnology sector. The city is ideally suited for such a technology-driven industry because of the presence of high-quality research and development facilities available here. This is a knowledge-based industry where close networking between research, academic institutions and industry is crucial for success. City based companies like Shantha Biotech, Bharat Biotech and Biological Evans – all pioneers in the field of biotechnology have hugely impacted the growth in this sector.

The setting up of the Genome Valley – the first state-of-the-art biotech cluster to facilitate life science research, training and manufacturing will thrust Hyderabad ahead as the global leader in the field of biotechnology. An important component of the Genome Valley is the ICICI Knowledge Park, committed to facilitate business-driven Research & Development in this sector.

The Biotech Parks will collaborate with research laboratories and technology parks in India and abroad and facilitate networking, technology transfers and formation of joint ventures etc.

Apollo

A great center for research and development

Hyderabad's rapid progress in the biotech sector is largely due to the presence of a large number of specialised research laboratories, which are all centers of excellence. Prominent among these are the Centre for Cellular and Molecular Biology (CCMB), Centre for DNA Fingerprinting and Diagnostics (CDFD), Indian Institute of Chemical Technology (IICT), International Crop Research Institute for Arid and Semi-Arid Tropics (ICRISAT), National Institute of Nutrition (NIN), Dr. Reddy's Research Foundation (DRF), ICICI Knowledge Park Ltd., Hyderabad Eye Research Foundation, Institute of Genetics and Hospital for Genetic Diseases and the Life Sciences Departments of the University of Hyderabad and Osmania University.

The Laboratory for the Conservation of Endangered Species (Lacones) is yet another state-of-the-art research center coming up in the city that will specialize in research on bio-diversity. This unique research project shall focus on such advanced studies like genetic characterisation, strategies for breeding, sperm and egg banks of endangered species, artificial insemination and in-vitro fertilization and eventually cloning of endangered animals.

With the convergence of the three sectors of information technology, biotechnology and pharma, Hyderabad is poised to make a giant leap as an icon of growth and development.

Knowledge city

The city has traditionally been an important training center for executives, bureaucrats and managers who come to hone their administrative and managerial skills. The prestigious Administrative Staff College of India, setup in 1956, is a pioneer in management education in India. It has trained over seventy five thousand middle and senior level managers from Indian and international corporate and government sector. The National Police Academy located in the suburbs, trains the rookies and senior officers of the prestigious Indian Police Service to lead and command the police force with skill and commitment. The GSI – Geological Survey of India, NISIET – National Institute of Small Industry Extension Training, the IIIT – The Indian Institute of Information Technology, NIFT – National institute of Fashion Technology are the other important teaching and training institutes in the city.

In the field of agriculture, the NG Ranga Agricultural University, MANAGE-National Institute of Agricultural Extension Management – a pioneer agricultural management institute in India, and ICRISAT-International Crops Research Institute for the Semi Arid Tropics, a UN body, collectively

The passing out parade
At the National Police Academy

The Union Home Minister,
Shri Shivraj Patil
greets young police officers at the NPA

Jubilant Graduates of ISB

provide managerial and technical skills to farmers, officers, managers and scientists in all sectors of agricultural economy and growth. These premier institutes are important centers for advanced research and development and aim to support farmers and fishermen in practicing 'sustainable agriculture'. NIRD or the National Institute of Rural Development is an apex institution associated with providing multi-disciplinary

HE President APJ Abdul Kalam interacts with students of NALSAR

research, consultancy and training in the field of rural development. Other than these premier training and research institutes, the city has six universities. The latest addition to the list is the prestigious Indian School of Business, built in partnership with the Kellogg School, Wharton School and the London School of Business. This reputed business school with its amazing infrastructure and faculty aspires to compete with the best international business schools. NALSAR University of Law or the National Academy of Legal Studies and Research is a national law school that is shaping to be India's premier institution for legal education.

Pioneer in defence research development

Hyderabad is home to the nation's premier Defence Research Development Organization-DRDO, which has made enormous contribution to the nation's conventional and nuclear weapons programme. India's prestigious Defence Research and Development Laboratories – DRDL, was established in the year 1961 under DRDO in the Kanchanbagh area of Hyderabad. The DRDL is largely responsible for the designing of the missile systems and Dr APJ Abdul Kalam, the President of India, popularly known as the father of the Indian Missile Technology, served as the Director of the institute.

DMRL – the Defence Metallurgical Research Laboratory conducts research on metallurgy and defence related materials and contributed largely to the development of the Agni Intermediary

DRDO
A-1
INDIA

Range Ballistic Missile. The NFC-Nuclear Fuel Complex caters to the fuel and zirconium requirement of the nation's nuclear power programme. Midhani is the center where a wide range of special metals and alloys using integrated and highly flexible manufacturing systems are manufactured for strategic sectors like space, defence, aeronautics and nuclear power. The NRSA – National Remote Sensing Agency is concerned with satellite mapping and the BDL or Bharat Dynamics Limited produces the most advanced guided missiles system for the Armed Forces. The DRDO along with the other institutions through their research and dedication has helped India achieve complete self reliance in its nuclear programme.

School kids get acquainted with missiles

Upgrading the City's infrastructure

For every macro attempt to beat Bangalore, which has been a tough competitor, there was a micro attempt to be distinctively unique. The coming of such major industries and institutions called for a major rehaul of the city's infrastructure. Roads were widened; power situation was overhauled and civic amenities upgraded. With the new Rajiv Gandhi International Airport coming up at Shamshabad, to be completed by 2008, Hyderabad is striding ahead of most Indian cities in the race for infrastructure development. To cope with the city's rapid expansion, Hyderabad Urban Development Authority, HUDA, has started work on the 160 km, eight lane ORR or the Outer Ring Road which will provide easy access to the Shamshabad International Airport, ease congestion within the city and help connect with nearly twenty five townships outside the city limits. The MRTS or the Metro Rail is another ambitious project on the anvil to be completed by 2009, which will smoothen the traffic and provide better public transport facility to the city dwellers.

Proposed Rajiv Gandhi International Airport

Among other smartening up measures, an effort was made to improve the air quality as well. Intensive plantation all over led to a cleaner and greener Hyderabad. An important achievement was the conservation of 356 precious acres of land belonging to the Nizam in the heart of the city. This property of the Nizam in the upscale Jubilee Hills was renamed Kasu Brahmanand Reddy Park and was given the status of a National Park. The only national park in the country to be located in the heart of the city, the KBR, untampered and untamed is a haven for innumerable species of flora and fauna today. A jogger's path was created around the KBR where every morning and evening thousands of health freaks throng for their daily dose of fresh air.

The Nehru Zoological Park considered the largest in the country spreads over three hundred acres and is home to around two hundred and fifty species of animals and birds. The Mrugvani National Park and the

Playfully yours, at the Nehru Zoological Park

Mahavir Harina Vanasthali National Parks are the other parks providing the essential lung space to the city.

Existing parks and commons were spruced up and new ones built. As a part of the Lake Conservation Project several water bodies that had deteriorated due to years of neglect and misuse like the Safilguda Lake were cleaned much to the relief of the people living in the neighbourhood. The Lotus Pond tucked away in the upscale Banjara Hills was another one saved in the nick of time and today supports an amazing botanical reserve and a prolific bird life. The pioneering effort of Hyderabad Urban Development Authority and the Municipal Corporation of Hyderabad in presenting a cleaner and greener Hyderabad, is laudable.

The Lotus Pond

Camera friendly at the Nehru Zoological Park

Tourism – from archaic to chic

Tourism had always been an important sector for the government – what with one hundred and thirty seven heritage buildings and thirty two heritage monuments in the city! The turn of the century saw a paradigm shift in this sector too. Hyderabad's new status as a global metro saw a sudden influx of tourists, executives, businessmen and students from India and abroad. A flurry of business activity brought in its wake a major expansion in the tourism and hospitality industry as well. While the traditional hot spots – Golconda, Charminar Salar Jung Museum and Lad Bazar were spruced up, tourists were offered newer and varied options. Hussain Sagar was cleaned and Necklace Road – a popular promenade along it, developed with walkways and fancy food joints. With the coming of Snow World, Eat Street and other theme parks around it, the Necklace Road is a popular hangout for the *Hyderabadis*.

City's glitterati enjoy a fashion show

Along Hussain Sagar

NTR Park

Shilparamam, an art and crafts village created on the outskirts is another popular destination in the city. Interestingly located on the same avenue as the Hitec city, Shilparamam is a symbol of ethnicity and the two together are iconic of Hyderabad – a heady blend of the old and the new! Durgam Cheruvu or the Secret Lake has been beautifully developed with gardens, walkways, restaurant and an arena. Today, a number of resorts on the outskirts provide perfect getaway for the harried city dwellers and visitors alike. Giving the city a jauntier tempo are the snazzy shopping malls, sleek multiplex theaters, pubs, lounge bars and lively coffee joints – the preferred rendezvous of both the young and the young at heart! These landmarks reiterate the changing temperament of Hyderabad from archaic to chic!

Durgum Cheruvu by night

The late 90's saw the opening of luxury star hotels and expansion of the existing ones. Convention Centers and Golf Courses came up. The newly inaugurated Hyderabad International Convention Center with state-of-the-art facilities is the first world class convention center in South Asia. Tie-ups with renowned international chains like Marriott and Radisson are in the offing, along with plans to add some more hotels to meet the flood of visitors to the city.

Hyderabad has moved on in ways more than one. While the traditional Industrial Exhibition Ground, or *Numaish*, at Nampally is still around, the ultra modern and futuristic – Hitex, built with German collaboration, presents the new face of Hyderabad. The Ministry of Tourism, Government of India adjudged the city as the best in terms of hospitality and tourism promotion for the year 2004, reaffirming Hyderabad's status as the new hotspot on the tourism map of India.

Children's day out at the BM Birla Science Center

Salarjung Museum

Tollywood – a major influence

Another industry that has hugely impacted the lives of the people of Andhra Pradesh is the Telugu film industry – popularly known as Tollywood. Right since Akkineni Nageswar Rao and NT RamaRao to Chiranjeevi, Venkatesh, Nagarjuna or Balakrishna, movie stars here are idolized like nowhere else in the country. The frenzy and emotion of the movie goers every Friday when a new film is released, is to be seen to be believed! On an average a hundred and fifteen films are made each year in Tollywood and the entertainment industry is worth more than five hundred crore today!

The Annapurna and Rama Naidu studios along with the high-tech Prasad Labs provide adequate infrastructure for film makers for production and post production works. Tollywood got a further fillip with the coming of the Ramoji Film City, a two thousand acre estate on the city outskirts. With Maya, a three hundred thousand square feet set preparation unit, state-of-the-art post production unit, film lab, digital film facility, world class cameras and scenic locales, the Ramoji Film City is a one stop destination for movie makers from India and even abroad.

Megastar Chiranjeevi

Cafes are a favourite haunt

Flirting with gastronomy

In the old, conservative Hyderabad, eating out was frowned upon. There were very few hotels and one of them was the Taj Mahal hotel in Abids. You had the usual 'tiffin centers' where people went for a snack or a meal which was essentially south Indian fare or the traditional *Hyderabadi biryani*. But the make over of the nineties' had the city flirt wildly with gastronomy. Modest eateries serving Andhra meal to *dhabas*, cafes, bistros, pubs and fancy restaurants serving gourmet fare today, you have it all in Hyderabad! South Indian tiffin centers coexist with Thai restaurants as do Mexican eateries with *Biryani* joints. Restauranteurs from Bombay, Bangalore and Delhi made a beeline to the city as business was good here. The exposure to a world beyond Hyderabad and the influx of young professionals from all over, has altered the city's foodscape from stubbornly staid to excitingly eclectic. Clubs too are a hot favourite. While the historic Secunderabad Club is the watering hole for the upper crust, the Nizam Club, Country Club and others are very popular.

Come evening and the city's bold and beautiful sashay into numerous pubs, trendy lounge bars and discotheques that dot the city.

The famous Madina Hotel in the old city

Art - the pulse of the city

Not just tourism, but the city has emerged as an important center for art and culture. With celebrated artists like Laxma Goud, Vaikuntham, Aziz, SuryaPrakash, Sisir Sahana, Late PT Reddy, DLN Reddy, Anjani Reddy and Lakshman Aeley among others making impressive contribution the national and international art scene, the art scape of the city has undergone a sea change. The coming of MF Hussain's Cinema Ghar along with several art galleries further widened the cultural horizon of Hyderabad. The newly opened State Art Gallery at Madhapur, with an amazing infrastructure endorses the proactive government policy towards promoting art and artists in the city.

Music too is an integral part of life here, as both serious and casual music lovers have a lot to choose from. Right from Rock to Carnatic and Hindustani classical, concerts, recitals and soirees are a regular feature in this music loving city. Auditorium and arenas like Ravindra Bharathi, Lalita Kala Thoranam and the new state-of-the-art Shilpa Kala Vedika regularly host cultural events, much to the delight of the *Hyderabadis*.

Vaikuntham and his Telengana women

The city sports a new look

National Games at Hyderabad

The new century re-energized the flagging spirit of the sporting community in Hyderabad. By successfully hosting the National Games and the Afro-Asian Games in 2003-04, the government spearheaded a sporting revolution that revitalized the sports infrastructure in the city. At GacchiBowli, on the outskirts, a games village was created with world class stadia, shooting ranges, swimming pools, hockey ground, gymnasium and numerous other training facilities. The existing Lal Bahadur Shastri Stadium and other sports and training centers were upgraded adding a new dimension to the city's growing stature as a world class metropolis. The whole nation admired as the glamorous ceremonies that preceded and followed the National and Afro Asian Games turned the city into a theater of supple art.

The Afro Asian Games

With such illustrious sports persons like Sania Mirza, Gopichand, VVS Laxman, Mythili Raj and others bringing acclaim, Hyderabad has proved that its infrastructure and facilities can compare with the best in the country and abroad.

Apart from serious sports, go-carting and bowling alleys have caught the fancy of the youngsters in the city. Racing, since the time of the Nizams continues to be a favourite sport of the city's elite. On weekends the race course buzzes with activity as avid racing fans get together for an exciting and fun-filled afternoon.

V V S Laxman

Sania Mirza

Times have changed and so has Hyderabad. The old charm is silenced, reduced to a collection of monuments and objects, muted and curated. In the garb of progress the new world has robbed the city of its rich essence. In many parts the scarred city stands uncovered, with all its warts on display – what with the unplanned growth, the nightmarish traffic and the disquieting pollution. The panacea lies in self restraint and a little less greed from all of us, those in power and those on the periphery.

But for all of us who love Hyderabad, its history is not over. With e-mails and digital cameras there is more of it than ever before. The drama and spectacle of today and the excitement of our times will be carried on and Hyderabad will continue to inspire all who will ever be touched by its magic and charm!

Clock Tower, Secunderabad

CHRONOLOGY

1591 Hyderabad is founded by Muhammad Quli Qutub Shah.

1591 Charminar is built by Muhammad Quli Qutub Shah.

1687 Golconda is captured by the Mughal army of Aurungzeb, signifying the end of the Qutub Shahi rule. The Mughals now control the kingdom .

1687 The capital of Deccan moves to Aurangabad.

1713 Nizam-ul-Mulk is appointed Governor of the six provinces of the Deccan.

1725 Nizam-ul-Mulk is conferred the title of Asif Jah by the Mughal Emperor Muhammad Shah.

1738 Nadir Shah invades India and Nizam-ul-Mulk mediates to negotiate peace.

1748 Nizam-ul-Mulk dies at the age of 77.

1748 After Nizam-ul-Mulk's death, the struggle for succession begins between his six sons.

1750 The Chowmahalla palace is built.

1751 Salabat Jung assumes the *Subedari* of Deccan.

1762 Nizam Ali Khan, Asif Jah II, becomes the *Subedar* or Governor of Deccan.

1763 Salabat Jung dies.

1763 During the reign of Nizam Ali Khan, Asif Jah II, Hyderabad once again becomes the capital of Deccan.

1798 The French General, Raymond dies.

1803 Nizam Ali Khan Asaf Jah II dies.

1803 The new Nizam is Sikander Jah, Asif Jah III.

1806 The twin city of Secunderabad is born and named after the new Nizam, Sikander Jah. Secunderabad was the second largest British cantonment in India.

1829 Sikander Jah, Asif Jah III dies.

1829 Nasir-ud-Daula is the new Nizam.

1853 The Treaty of Berar is signed by which the administration of the district of Berar is handed over to the British.

1857 Nasir-ud Daula dies and Afzal-ud-Daula, Asif Jah V, is the fifth Nizam.

1857 The First War of Independence begins. The floundering Mughal Empire finally collapses.

1861 The 'Order of Star of India' is conferred on Afzal-ud-Daula, the fifth Nizam.

1869 The fifth Nizam dies.

1869 The two year old prince, Mir Mahboob Ali Khan, is proclaimed the new Nizam.

1869 The Nizam State Railway is set up.

1876 The practice of 'Sati' or the self immolation of Hindu widow is banned in the state.

1879 The Malakpet Race Course opens.

1883 Prime Minister, Salar Jung I, passes away.

1884 Work starts on Falaknuma.

The background is a picture of a jadi taken at Paigah Tombs

1890 The Asifia State Library is established.

1892 Lord and Lady Lansdowne visit Hyderabad.

1893 Archduke Franz Ferdinand of Austria visits Hyderabad.

1895 Lord and Lady Elgin visit Hyderabad.

1897 Sir Ronald Ross discovers the malarial parasite.

1902 Lord and Lady Curzon visit Hyderabad.

1905 The foundation of the Town Hall or the present day Legislative Assembly is laid by Mahboob Ali Khan, Asif Jah VI.

1908 Widespread devastation due to the Musi floods.

1908 The Nizamia Observatory is established.

1911 Mahboob Ali Pasha, the sixth Nizam, dies.

1911 Mir Osman Ali Khan is proclaimed the seventh Nizam of Hyderabad.

1914 The Department of Archaeology is setup.

1915 Construction of the High Court begins and ends in 1919.

1917 Osmania University is established.

1919 Nizam VII introduces the Executive Council.

1920 Osman Sagar is constructed followed by Himayat Sagar in 1927.

1921 The executive and judiciary are separated.

1922 Prince of Wales visits Hyderabad.

1923 The Jagirdar College, or the present day Hyderabad Public School is established.

1926 Osmania Medical College is established.

1929 The Industrial Trust Fund is established to promote industrial growth.

1931 Prince Azam Jah and Prince Moazzam Jah are married in Nice, France to Princess DurruShehvar and Princess Niloufer, the daughter and niece of the Caliph of Turkey.

1936 Hyderabad State Aero Club is established at Begumpet.

1937 Nizam VII celebrates his Silver anniversary or 25 years of his reign.

1947 India gains Independence.

1947 The last British resident leaves Hyderabad.

1947 The Standstill Agreement signed with the Government of India.

1948 The government of India initiates Police Action against Hyderabad.

1948 Military rule is imposed. The Asif Jahi rule comes to an end and Hyderabad merges with the Union of India.

1950 Mir Osman Ali Khan, the seventh Nizam is appointed the *Rajpramukh* of the state a position that he holds till 1956.

1956 The State of Andhra Pradesh is formed with Hyderabad as its capital.

1967 Mir Osman Ali Khan dies.

The background is a picture of a jadli taken at Paigah Tombs

SELECT BIBLIOGRAPHY

Hyderabad 400 years
– Raza Ali Khan

City of Legends The story of Hyderabad
– Ian Austen

The Splendour of Hyderabad
– Dr M A Nayeem

Glimpses of the Nizam's Dominion
– Compiled by AClaude Campbell

Pictorial Hyderabad
– K Krishnaswamy Mudiraj

Golconda and Hyderabad
– Shehbaz H Safrani (Ed)

Hyderabad: The Power of Glory
– Deccan Books

Images of Hyderabad
– 'Siyasat' Publication

Andhra Pradesh District Gazetteer
– Hyderabad

Hyderabad-Memoirs of a City
– Narendra Luther

Cities of India – Hyderabad
– Narendra Luther

The Rockitecture of Andhra Pradesh
– Narendra Luther

The White Mughals
– William Darlymple

Under the Charminar
– William Darlymple

Hyderabad: 400 Glorious Years
– K Chandriah

The essential Andhra cook book
– Bilkis I Latif

Andhra Pradesh – Maa Telugu Talli

Hyderabad 2020 – A Plan for Sustainable Development HUDA

Outlook Traveller August 2004

Jetwings April 2005 Vol 5

Intach magazine Various issues

Times of India

VISUAL CREDITS

Chapter 4 & 5
Jagdish and Kamla Mittal
Museum of Indian Art.

Old Pictures
Siyasat Library
Dept. of Archives, Govt of A.P.
Salarjung Museum
Museum at Purani Haveli
Insignia, raffle ticket, map, buckle, receipt, driving license: AN Medhora

New Visuals
D Ravinder Reddy
Ravi Press Photo
6-3-902/7/4. Somajiguda,
Hyderabad - 500 082
ravistudios@gmail.com
+91-40-9866332244

Picture of a jaali taken at Paigah Tombs